At Issue

I Biofuels

Margaret Haerens, Book Editor

GREENHAVEN PRESS
A part of Gale, Cengage Learning

GALE
CENGAGE Learning·

Detroit • New York • San Francisco • New Haven, Conn • Waterville, Maine • London

GALE
CENGAGE Learning·

Elizabeth Des Chenes, *Director, Publishing Solutions*

© 2012 Greenhaven Press, a part of Gale, Cengage Learning.

Gale and Greenhaven Press are registered trademarks used herein under license.

For more information, contact:
Greenhaven Press
27500 Drake Rd.
Farmington Hills, MI 48331-3535
Or you can visit our Internet site at gale.cengage.com

For product information and technology assistance, contact us at

Gale Customer Support, 1-800-877-4253
For permission to use material from this text or product, submit all requests online at www.cengage.com/permissions

Further permissions questions can be e-mailed to permissionrequest@cengage.com

Articles in Greenhaven Press anthologies are often edited for length to meet page requirements. In addition, original titles of these works are changed to clearly present the main thesis and to explicitly indicate the author's opinion. Every effort is made to ensure that Greenhaven Press accurately reflects the original intent of the authors. Every effort has been made to trace the owners of copyrighted material.

Cover image copyright, Debra Hughes 2007. Used under license from Shutterstock.com.

LIBRARY OF CONGRESS CATALOGING-IN-PUBLICATION DATA

Biofuels / Margaret Haerens, book editor.
    p. cm. -- (At issue)
    Summary: "Biofuels: Books in this anthology series focus a wide range of viewpoints onto a single controversial issue, providing in-depth discussions by leading advocates, a quick grounding in the issues, and a challenge to critical thinking skills"-- Provided by publisher.
    Includes bibliographical references and index.
    ISBN 978-0-7377-5552-7 (hardback) -- ISBN 978-0-7377-5553-4 (pbk.)
    1. Biomass energy--Economic aspects. 2. Biomass energy--United States. I. Haerens, Margaret.
    HD9502.5.B542B553 2012
    333.95'39--dc23
                                                    2012007090

Printed in the United States of America
    1 2 3 4 5   16 15 14 13 12
ED150

Contents

Introduction

Biofuels are a renewable fuel source derived from biomass or biowaste. Also known as agrofuel, biofuels have been made from a variety of biomass sources throughout history, including agricultural crops such as corn and switchgrass as well as algae, animal fat, and vegetable oil. Energy can also be derived from biowaste, such as landfill gases (LFG), emitted from rotting garbage in landfills. In fact, it is thought that biofuel can be produced from any carbon source. The challenge, however, is to convert the biomass energy safely, cleanly, and efficiently into the liquid fuel that powers the automobiles, planes, trains, and other transportation that keeps economies around the world growing.

In the past few decades, the popularity of biofuels has skyrocketed. One of the main reasons is that biofuels are a much cleaner form of energy than fossil fuels and thereby have a smaller impact on the environment. Another reason that countries like the United States are so intent on researching and developing biofuels is that a transition to such fuels would reduce American dependence on foreign oil, thereby strengthening both the US economy and national security.

The use of biofuels can be traced back to the dawn of human history, when men and women discovered fire. Wood is considered the first biofuel: a renewable source of energy that cooked food and provided warmth for the human race. Another early use of biofuel was the process used by the Sumerians, an ancient people who lived in what is now Iraq, to ferment grainstarch in order to brew beer. In fact, the fermentation process used by the Sumerians to brew beer also forms the basis of ethanol production. A volatile, colorless liquid, ethanol has been popular throughout history as an intoxicating but dangerous alcoholic beverage. In the United States, it is called grain alcohol. Although it can be traced back to the era of the ancient Greeks and Romans, the first recorded case of grain alcohol production from distilled wine took place in Italy in the twelfth century. In 1796 Johann Tobias Lowitz was the first to filter distilled alcohol through charcoal to get pure ethanol, and by 1826, it was being produced synthetically.

It did not take long for scientists to discover the benefits of ethanol as a fuel. It was quickly utilized as a fuel for lamps, and because it produced no smoke as it burned, by the 1840s, ethanol was being widely used as a lamp fuel across Europe and the United States. However, a draconian tax levied on industrial alcohol production during the Civil War led to a precipitous decline in ethanol use in the late-nineteenth century in America. The tax was repealed in 1906—right in time for the advent of the automobile.

In 1893 a German engineer named Rudolf Diesel developed a type of motor, known as the diesel engine, which ran on peanut oil. Anticipating the use of biofuels like peanut oil to run automobiles instead of gas, the American inventor Henry Ford designed his first Model T to run on ethanol in 1908. For years, Ford pushed ethanol as the most logical fuel for his automobiles. However, rising corn prices combined with a huge supply of domestic oil resulted in gasoline becoming the preferred fuel source for the American automobile. The situation for ethanol worsened in the United States during Prohibition (1920–1933), when the production of ethanol became linked with making moonshine and bootlegging.

Nonetheless, there were those who would not give up on ethanol. For example, Henry Ford continued to advocate for biofuels, even building an ethanol production plant in Kansas. The American scientist and inventor George Washington Carver believed that agricultural crops such as peanuts, soybeans, and sweet potatoes could be utilized not just as an inexpensive food source for needy families but also as biofuels, cosmetics, paints, dyes, and other helpful products.

During World War II, chronic gas shortages led to the popularity of ethanol-gasoline blends. In Germany, inventors combined ethanol made from potatoes with gasoline to extend fuel supplies. In England, it became common to use an ethanol-gasoline blend during the war. In the post-war period, however, Middle Eastern oil producers lowered the price of gasoline, making it affordable again. The lower prices also killed off much of the demand for biofuels among consumers and stalled most of the research in the field.

In the late 1970s a worldwide oil crisis renewed interest in biofuels as an alternative to oil. Companies reintroduced ethanol-gasoline blends to the US market, and for a fleeting time it was thought that ethanol could replace gasoline in American transportation and effectively end US dependence on Middle East oil. However, after the crisis passed, consumers went back to using gasoline. Several major oil companies continued to distribute the blends, however, and one of these, known as E10, is still used widely.

Over the last few decades, environmental activists, scientists, and oil companies have begun to realize that it is imperative to develop cost-efficient, clean, and renewable biofuels. Study after study showed that fossil fuels like oil and coal were polluting the air, land, and water and were considered prime causes of climate change. Further, the supply and price of gasoline was dependent on the US relationship with Middle East oil producers, a relationship that was often complicated by geopolitical issues. Many political and economic experts came to the realization that the US needed to invest in the development of biofuels as a way to transition away from oil and to a clean, renewable, and domestic source of fuel.

Biofuels are also seen as a way to boost the American agricultural sector. Whether it is corn, jatropha seeds, or switchgrass, many of the various sources of biofuels can be grown and processed in the US. Biofuel production from biowaste can also address the disposal problems many municipalities have with garbage and industrial waste. Scientists are busily researching and developing technology to safely, cleanly, and efficiently convert waste into biofuels.

It is widely believed that biofuels will become a major component of the world's energy future; with the world's limited oil supply, it is essential to transition to a renewable fuel source that is energy efficient and environmentally sound. Such a transition is not without controversies, however. The viewpoints presented in *At Issue: Biofuels* examine these debates and provide insight into many aspects of the issues surrounding a number of emerging and established biofuels.

1

Biofuels Hold Both Risks and Opportunities

Suzanne Hunt

Suzanne Hunt is an independent consultant to the US Department of Energy.

In recent years, there has been a significant backlash against first-generation biofuels, especially corn-based ethanol and biodiesel. It is a valid concern because increased farming and production of biofuels have negative environmental consequences. However, the development of alternative sources for biofuel production holds many social and environmental opportunities and requires a rational approach. Second-generation biofuels have tremendous potential to transcend the key limitations of first-generation biofuels.

Many people had never heard of biofuels two years ago, yet now they are receiving a lot of publicity—much of it negative. Initially, political and business circles touted the potential benefits of biofuels; it was a speechwriter's dream. Here was an energy source that promised jobs, rural revitalization, and greater independence from foreign oil producers.

At a time of growing anxiety over global warming, biofuels promised a clean, liquid transport fuel that would help reduce levels of greenhouse gas emissions. According to the Intergovernmental Panel on Climate Change Fourth Assessment Report in early 2007, an estimated 1.8–4 degree Celsius rise in

Suzanne Hunt, "Biofuels, Neither Saviour nor Scourge: The Case for a Selective Strategy," *World Policy Journal*, March 22, 2008. worldpolicy.org. Copyright © 2008 by SAGE Publications. All rights reserved. Reproduced by permission.

global temperatures is likely by the end of the century, if no dramatic change in energy supply and use occurs globally. The report further confirmed that, given the current state of scientific knowledge, it is 90 percent certain that the emissions caused by humans are responsible for the increasing warming of the planet's surface. Studies of climate patterns conclude with increased certainty that a continuing rise in greenhouse gas levels in the atmosphere will most likely result in a variety of alarming—and quite possibly catastrophic—climate impacts.

In European Union member states, Japan, and a number of other countries that have signed the Kyoto Protocol [an international treaty that aims to address climate change], concern about climate change has been a powerful policy driver for the biofuels industry. (Currently, transport fuels account for about a quarter of energy-related greenhouse gas emissions.)

[A] number of factors increasingly make reliance on petroleum a risky proposition. . . .

More Benefits of Biofuels

Meanwhile, with soaring gas prices and U.S. troops engaged in a war overseas, biofuels promised the added benefit of a secure, domestic energy source. The global transport system is almost entirely dependent on petroleum derivatives, and thus highly vulnerable. Leaving aside the complicated question of peak oil, a number of factors increasingly make reliance on petroleum a risky proposition: petro-states such as Iran and Venezuela may threaten to cut production, continued conflict in the oil-rich Middle East may impede the flow of oil, and low global refining capacity creates dangerous bottlenecks in the current fuel system that leaves us susceptible to natural disasters and malicious attacks.

Add to this a moral component: the world is all but certain to struggle with the intertwined challenges of energy security and climate change, but it is humanity's poor who will suffer most, as they tend to live in regions most vulnerable to extreme weather events, often lack the means for secure shelter and transport, and are most affected by increased food prices and shrinking energy supplies. Globally, some 2.4 billion people rely on traditional biomass sources (firewood, oil, coal) for energy; and some 1.6 billion lack access to electricity. Without new energy solutions, 1.4 billion people will still lack electricity by 2030, the majority living in South Asia and sub-Saharan Africa. Some regions, notably the Caribbean, are almost completely dependent on imported petroleum for all of their energy needs. In these regions, even small amounts of domestically-produced biofuels can help diversify fuel options, thereby reducing risk and vulnerability.

With all these potential benefits, the biofuels market has grown by leaps and bounds over the past few years. There were some voices of caution during this giddy growth period, but they were largely unheeded. Just as popular sentiment had moved behind biofuels, it abruptly shifted course at an equally dizzying pace. The speed of the sea change in public opinion was shocking. Biofuels went from national savior to deadly scam in a matter of months. As wheat, corn, and rice prices reached new peaks this spring, the food riots that spread through poorer countries in Asia, Africa, and the Caribbean have been increasingly linked in public debate to biofuels.

Just as popular sentiment had moved behind biofuels, it abruptly shifted course at an equally dizzying pace.

The Biofuels Conundrum

Biofuels are neither a panacea nor a scourge. It is a valid concern that increased farming and production of biofuels are beginning to add pressure to stressed natural systems and failing social systems. It is clear that we need to develop energy alternatives, and quickly. The first and generally most cost-effective option is, and always should be, to reduce the consumption of petroleum through much more aggressive efficiency requirements, the development of light-weight materials for cars and trucks, improved battery technologies, new energy storage mechanisms, and the promotion of public transport. Biofuels belong within this portfolio of solutions. In total, biofuels today account for less than 2 percent of liquid transport fuels. This may seem like a small share, but biofuels have met about 30 percent of the growth in global demand for liquid transport fuels over the past three years [2005 to 2008]. That is a significant contribution to the balance of the market.

[A] second generation of advanced biofuels holds enormous potential to break through some of the key limitations of current fuels.

In the European Union [EU], for example, the 27 member states are currently required by law to meet volumetric biofuels targets. A target approved in 2003 stipulated that 5.75 percent of member states' fuel supplies must be composed of biofuels by 2010; this was followed in 2007 by a blending mandate calling for renewable fuels to make up 10 percent of transport fuel supply by 2020. But if the member states revoke this requirement, as a growing chorus suggests—rather than attaching sustainability standards—they will have no influence over now biofuels are produced.

With biofuels, as with all energy resources, there are trade-offs and risks, but there are also opportunities. The challenge today is to deal rationally with this energy source by developing effective safeguards against the risks and capitalizing on the social and environmental opportunities.

A Biofuel Primer

The two most common biofuels today are ethanol (made from starchy crops like sugarcane and corn) and biodiesel (which is generally derived from vegetable oils or animal fats). Ethanol is either blended with gasoline in low concentrations as an oxygenate or used at higher concentrations in Flex Fuel Vehicles (FFVs) that are designed to run on either unleaded gasoline or any blend of up to 85 percent ethanol. In the United States today, about half the gasoline sold at the pump is already 10 percent ethanol. Biodiesel can be used in diesel engines in either its pure form or as a blend with conventional diesel fuel. While these fuels hold significant potential to reduce greenhouse gas emissions and curb the global appetite for carbon-based petroleum products, there is now some concern over the emissions produced in the growing and refining of these fuels, as well as land-use issues, and their complex effect on food and grain prices.

But a second generation of advanced biofuels holds enormous potential to break through some of the key limitations of current fuels. Advanced biofuels (biobutanol and synthetic diesel, for example) and other biofuels derived from switchgrass, garbage, and algae are now under development in America, Europe, China, and elsewhere. Meanwhile, new conversion technologies are expected to expand production potential by allowing for the use of an array of non-food biomass sources, which will greatly improve net greenhouse gas emissions and generate other positive environmental impacts.

Ethanol use, today's principal biofuel, has grown by some 12 percent annually over the past seven years, more than doubling its production. Still, biofuels currently account for less than 2 percent of global transport fuels and well below 1 percent of world agricultural land. Most ethanol is produced in the United States and Brazil, which together account for three-quarters of world output. In Brazil, ethanol comprises nearly 50 percent of the fuel at the pump. The United States produces more ethanol than Brazil, but total percentage at the pump domestically is still less than 5 percent due to our massive fuel consumption. Biodiesel production has grown by 700 percent since 2000—largely in Europe—but total volume is still only about 10 percent of global ethanol production.

In the broader scope of global biomass utilization, liquid biofuels for transportation are but a tiny fraction of the whole. The majority of organic matter (or biomass) is used for animal feed, food, consumer goods and building materials, with only a small percentage devoted specifically toward energy generation—and even less used to produce liquid biofuels. Still, there is considerable concern over the global rush to produce biofuels and it is critical to disaggregate the true issues from the din of the debate.

Concern #1: Food Prices

Perhaps the most emotionally charged aspect of the developing debate concerns the link between biofuels and food prices. While many have been quick to blame biofuels for current high commodity prices, the true picture is inherently more complex. As a report by the International Energy Agency notes, "it is true that increased use of biofuels has contributed to recent increases in grains and vegetable oils. But other factors, such as recent droughts and surging demand for meat and milk products in Asia have probably played a significantly larger role." A closer look at current key drivers of food prices is instructive.

For a start, soaring petroleum prices have contributed to record-high fertilizer and diesel prices for farmers, with spillover increases in the costs of production, packaging, and distribution that continue along the chain from farm to supermarket. Further, there has been a shift towards high-protein diets in fast developing countries, notably China and India. Meat production has thus increased, and as livestock numbers have swelled, greater inputs of feed and grain are required. It is commonly forgotten that approximately 40 percent of the world's grain is used to feed animals, not people. Add to this relatively low inventories of key commodities such as wheat and corn—in part due to severe droughts in major wheat producing countries, such as Australia—and it is easy to see why the global market now faces low supply and high demand. Finally, as the majority of commodities are traded in U.S. dollars, a weakened currency has made imports more expensive. Speculation in the oil market (and some believe in the food commodity markets) is also driving up prices.

Some Perspective on Fuel Prices

But to fully disentangle the biofuel reality from the current debate, it is also important to differentiate between commodities. Many of the recent food riots across the globe have been in protest of spiking rice prices. Rice, though, is not used to make biofuels, nor is the land in which rice is grown generally suitable for such biofuel crops as corn and soy. Of the 13.2 billion hectares of the global total land area, 1.5 billion hectares are used to produce arable crops and 3.5 billion hectares are used as pasture for meat, milk, and wool production. Crops currently used specifically for biofuels utilize about 25 million hectares of land worldwide, only about 0.5 percent of agricultural acreage. In Brazil, for example, ethanol produced from sugarcane (which constitutes nearly 50 percent of total gasoline demand) is grown on just 1 percent of the 320 million hectares of arable land and pasture.

In the U.S. market, about 25 percent of corn production currently is used for ethanol, slightly more than the amount of corn that the United States exports. Globally, ethanol and biodiesel production now consume about 4 percent of the world's grain. This would suggest that biofuels produced from food crops have a similarly small influence on grain prices a fact recently seconded by economists at the U.S. Department of Agriculture. Currently, there is little flexibility in commodity markets, and, with inelastic supply and demand curves, short-term disproportionate impacts and price fluctuations are increasingly common. As the National Resource Defense Council's Nathanael Greene put it, "economic modeling confirms that biofuels are a modest part of the food price picture." Nevertheless, although analyses show that currently biofuels are not a significant cause of food price increases, rapid growth in grain use for biofuels in the future may become an important factor.

Concern #2: Land Use

One of the latest rounds in the biofuels debate centers on greenhouse gas emissions from indirect land-use changes. Currently, biofuels are made predominantly from food crops. But while biofuels account for a small fraction of total agricultural acreage, new fields and land are being cleared to produce biofuels and meet market demand. Increased cultivation adds pressure to already stressed ecosystems, requiring more land, water, and other natural resources. Perhaps the most urgent risk is the threat posed to native ecosystems, such as forests, that store massive amounts of carbon. In addition to disturbing wildlife, soils, and hydrological and nutrient cycles, the conversion of rainforest and native prairies to agricultural land releases enormous amounts of carbon—both from burning vegetation to clear fields and from tilling soil.

While current policy mechanisms are relatively efficacious in mitigating the direct impacts of biofuels production (for example, water pollution regulations on agricultural production in the United States would also apply to biofuels production), indirect impacts present a significant challenge, both to scientists and policymakers. Take one example: if American farmers begin to plant more corn for biofuels and less soy, it is likely that the global soy price will rise, creating added incentive for farmers in other parts of the world to increase soy production. Increased production can be achieved by increasing yields, expanding into new land, or substituting for other crops. The effects can be deleterious: increased pesticides and chemical inputs, wholesale clearing of land and native forests for biofuel feed-stock cultivation, and crop displacement can dramatically increase greenhouse gas emissions. Thus, the calculus for assessing the indirect impact of, say, the growth in U.S. corn production for ethanol on global agriculture—and the associated greenhouse gas emissions—are enormously complex.

Recent articles in the authoritative journal *Science* on greenhouse gas emissions from land-use change caused indirectly from biofuels production have received wide attention. These articles have argued that virtually all biofuels produced today will result in more, not less, greenhouse gas emissions than the current use and production of fossil fuels. This has focused attention on a key issue, but it is important to realize that this field of research is very new—these studies are among the first ever peer-reviewed articles attempting to quantify greenhouse gas emissions impacts of indirect land-use changes. As such, many of the underlying assumptions are being questioned and the adequacy of the models and datasets used are being challenged. Numerous research efforts are underway around the world to better understand these land-use and greenhouse gas emission dynamics.

Thus, while biofuels offer significant potential for greenhouse gas emission reductions, there are risks. Even among current types of biofuels there exists a wide range in net emissions impacts. Some may indeed generate net increases in greenhouse gas emissions. Thus, it is critical that, as our understanding progresses, we begin to take a full life-cycle account of biofuel agriculture and production, including direct and indirect land-use changes, feed-stock type, agricultural practices, energy replacement options, conversion and refining processes, and end use. Putting aside for a moment the potential greenhouse gas emissions from indirect land-use change, conventional corn-based ethanol is believed to produce roughly 15–35 percent net greenhouse gas emission reduction; soy-based biodiesel results in a net greenhouse gas emission reduction of 30–50 percent; cellulosic ethanol generates net greenhouse gas emissions reductions of 70–90 percent; and Brazilian sugar cane ethanol reduces net greenhouse emissions by 80–90 percent. These are considerable gains.

Moving Forward

As petroleum-based fuels still dominate global markets, alternative sources require a significant push in order to gain a foothold. Biofuels are multi-sectoral products that require a much higher degree of logistical coordination and more sophisticated planning. They must integrate into agricultural and forestry systems with appropriate agronomic and harvesting practices. They require appropriate collection, production, distribution, and end-use infrastructure (i.e., compatibility with automobile engines and manufacturer warrantees, ability to blend with other fuels, appropriate fuel pumps, distribution systems, pipelines, etc.). But this is the simple stuff. Biofuels production affects the transport and energy industries, agriculture and rural development, and global trade—all of which make the policy environment inherently complex. And, as public pressure is stoked by an increasingly shrill debate, the political stakes of biofuel policies are raised.

In much of the developing world, biofuels industries are in their nascent stages and regulatory regimes have yet to be developed. We can, however, use lessons learned in the handful of countries that maintain well-developed biofuels industries. While experiences in Brazil, the United States, and Europe over the past few decades are not necessarily transferable to other regions, they can be instructive. Voluntary or mandatory blending targets have been a powerful means of instigating and accelerating the development of biofuels industries. Mandates have been accompanied by various combinations of tax incentives, preferential government purchasing, and other price supports. For example, in the much studied Brazil experience, the government is requiring that the state oil company, Petrobras, preferentially purchase biodiesel feed-stock from small farmers. Government-supported research and development, grants, loans, guarantees, and other direct financial supports have also played an import role in biofuels development. And public-private partnerships have proven very effective. In the United States, for example, the Department of Energy spent roughly $1 billion in 2007 with the goal of helping companies develop next-generation biofuels technologies and bring processes and products to the market.

Sustainability Assurance Efforts

The risk that biofuels production will cause environmental harm has prompted a range of sustainability assurance efforts. Individual government efforts in Europe (especially in the Netherlands, the United Kingdom, and Germany) have lead to more coordinated effort including proposed EU-wide mandatory sustainability requirements for biofuels. In 2005, the advanced industrial nations comprising the Group of Eight (G8) called for the creation of a Global Bioenergy Partnership (GBEP) to facilitate international collaboration on bioenergy and energy security, food security, and environmental sustainability. While achieving consensus among the member governments of GBEP has been difficult, the development of a sustainability assurance framework is underway. Notably, GBEP's greenhouse gas accounting task force has provided a vital forum for scientists and governments from member countries to share strategies to measure and account for the greenhouse gas emissions implications of biofuels. These efforts have informed new proposed European legislation that will likely feature a list of compulsory "sustainability criteria," including land-use and biodiversity requirements: for example, biofuels and other bioliquids would not be made from "raw materials obtained from land with recognized high biodiversity value" or from land with high carbon stocks. At the time of writing, a 35 percent or higher greenhouse gas emissions reductions requirement for biofuels was also being debated.

[B]iofuels industries are in their nascent stages and regulatory regimes have yet to be developed.

Sustainability is also being discussed is the International Biofuels Forum (IBF), a collaboration platform for the world's biggest biofuels producers and consumers: Brazil, China, India, South Africa, the United States, and the European Union. These nations are beginning to turn their attention to the need to develop sustainable biofuels. However, their efforts to date have primarily focused on international biofuel market development and the harmonization of technical standards and codes.

Bilateral Agreements

In addition to the ongoing multilateral discussions, a number of bilateral agreements have been signed between countries to advance biofuels development. The United States and China, Germany and China, and the United States and Brazil, have all signed bilateral memorandums of understanding related to the sustainable development of biofuels, and to foster collaboration around advanced production and market expansion. But there are as yet no international, multilateral binding regulations for biofuels that address such potential negative social and environmental impacts of biofuels as habitat conversion, water and air pollution, and land-use conflicts.

The primary concern is that, without international standards and cooperation, a biofuels free-for-all could develop that would pay little regard to sustainability and environmental concerns. Due to the rapid growth of the biofuels industry, and in the absence of strong national or international policy frameworks, a number of approaches to building a robust and sustainable global industry have been suggested, including several non-traditional policy options. One option is the creation of a multilateral environmental agreement (MEA) for biofuels. However, given the non-binding nature of such agreements, the standards are not likely to be rigorous. Another way forward would be to integrate sustainable biofuel standards into existing international systems like the International Standards Organization (ISO) which has traditionally focused on certifying technical standards for industry but has some sustainability focused initiatives. The European Standardization Organization (CEN) is exploring the role that ISO might play in sustainability assurances for biofuels and has recently launched its own EU "Sustainable Bioenergy Standards" initiative.

Adding to the effort, in March 2008, a Sustainable Biofuels Consensus was developed by a group of global specialists at the Rockefeller Foundation Bellagio Center in Italy. These experts crafted a vision for the sustainable production, use, and trade of transport biofuels and made a number of specific recommendations to policymakers. (Full disclosure: I was among the specialists invited to contribute to the Bellagio group.) The Consensus recommends better integrating and coordinating national policy frameworks; rigorously assessing and mitigating negative impacts of biofuels trade, use, and production; building a system to reward positive impacts and investments; encouraging Informed dialogues to build consensus for new projects; increasing investment in research, development, and demonstration; and making sure that trade policies and climate change policies work In concert. It is an ambitious but hopeful agenda.

2

The New Generation of Biofuels Are Superior to Fossil Fuels

Frances Cerra Whittelsey

Frances Cerra Whittelsey is an author and journalist.

Biofuels have been hit with a wave of criticism because, as some experts charge, they drive up food prices, destroy rain forests, and escalate the problem of climate change. However, biofuels are certainly a far better option than continued dependence on fossil fuels. One solution to the problem is encouraging people to eat less meat; raising animals for food devours resources and drives climate change. A more feasible option is developing a new generation of biofuels, using switchgrass, slash, and algae. The US government needs to effectively support these innovations, which show great potential in addressing the country's energy needs.

Only three years ago [2005] there was such a surplus of corn in the Midwest that it became a joke. Someone pasted the image of a skier into a photo of a mountainous pile of the stuff, labeled it "Ski Iowa," and e-mailed it around the Internet to hand everyone a laugh—except the farmers, of course. At the time, turning all that unwanted corn into ethanol to replace gasoline seemed like a great idea.

But that was then. Today, corn ethanol has become the bad-boy alternative to petroleum, criticized for driving up food prices, destroying rain forests and worsening climate change. For good measure, the criticism is usually leveled at biofuels in general, even though the other category of biofuel—biodiesel—is not made from corn and has a much more beneficial climate-improving profile. For some environmentalists, the only acceptable green energy options are wind, solar and geothermal power. Former Vice President Al Gore recently challenged America to end our reliance on carbon-based fuels in ten years by shifting electricity production to those three ideal options. Along the way, he suggested assisting auto makers to build plug-in cars and phase out gasoline and diesel-powered vehicles.

However, even if this Utopia can be achieved in a decade—and I fervently hope that it can—Americans are stuck with cars they wish they could plug in but can't. America and the world will need liquid fuels for a long time to come, and biofuels, including some corn ethanol made at the most efficient distilleries, offer a far better option than continued use of fossil fuels.

A False Choice

Biofuel critics, including the Grocery Manufacturers of America, often frame the problem as a choice between feeding people and feeding SUVs; they blame rising food prices on diverting food crops to fuel production. The trade group has mounted a public relations campaign to try to roll back high Congressional mandates for increasing use of ethanol. While concern about rising food prices is certainly justified, for grocery manufacturers the argument is also self-serving. Food manufacturers make their profits not on raw vegetables or commodities like cooking oil but on processed foods, and they want to direct public anger about food price inflation away from themselves. Packaging, processing, advertising, transportation and profits account for most of the price of processed foods, and the surging price of oil figures heavily in that mix. The cost of corn, even as the major ingredient in a food like corn flakes, accounts for a tiny fraction of the final price.

But it's false to frame the biofuel debate as a choice between people or SUVs. While there are daily references in the media to the diversion of corn to fuel-making, there's hardly ever a mention of the fact that feeding our livestock uses 50 percent to 60 percent of the American corn crop. Here are the calculations used by the US Agriculture Department's Economic Research Service for how much corn animals must be fed to produce a pound of meat for retail sale: seven pounds of corn equals one pound of beef; six-and-a-half pounds of corn equals one pound of pork; two and six-tenths pounds of corn equals one pound of chicken. (Meat industry estimates are lower but generally refer to the amount of corn necessary to make the live animal gain a pound, not the amount necessary to get a pound of food in the meat case.) Corn is a dietary staple in parts of the world like Mexico, but not here in the United States, where the answer to "What's for dinner?" is supposed to be "beef." Talk about feeding SUVs or people is deceptive, since it masks the intermediate step of feeding animals a whole lot of corn to get one steak dinner.

America and the world will need liquid fuels for a long time to come, and biofuels, including some corn ethanol made at the most efficient distilleries, offer a far better option than continued use of fossil fuels.

Even more hidden from public view is the role of animal feeding in global warming. The shocking fact is that production of beef, pork and poultry is a bigger part of the climate problem than the cars and trucks we drive, indeed of the whole transportation sector. In our fantasies—and ads—we see contented cows eating grass, but the fact is all but a lucky few spend much of their lives in dismal feedlots where grass does not grow, getting fat on corn and other unspeakable byproducts. Internationally, two-thirds of the earth's available agricultural land is used to raise animals and their feed crops, primarily corn and soybeans, and the trend is accelerating as people in Latin America and Asia increasingly demand an Americanized diet rich in meat. The need to grow more animal feed and more animals has been devastating rainforests and areas like Brazil's Cerrado region, the world's most biologically diverse savannah, long before the demand for biofuels began escalating.

It's What We Eat

Vegetarians have long understood this issue, but asking the American public to eat less meat is still a radical idea, politically untouchable. Yet the meat industry is a giant source of greenhouse gases, of which carbon dioxide is only one, and not the most dangerous one. All those steer feedlots and factory buildings crammed with pigs and chickens produce immense amounts of animal wastes that give off methane. On an equivalent basis to carbon dioxide, methane is twenty-three times more potent as a greenhouse gas. When you add in the production of fertilizer and other aspects of animal farming (including land use changes, feed transport, etc.) livestock farming is responsible for nearly one-fifth of human-induced greenhouse gas emissions, more than the transportation sector, according to a 2006 report by the Food and Agriculture Organization of the United Nations.

None of which excuses knocking down trees in a rain forest to grow fuel crops or burning dirty coal to make a supposedly cleaner, biofuel substitute. People around the world for whom corn and other grains are a food staple—not an ingredient or animal feed—need help to avoid starvation, regardless of the reason, be it biofuel production, drought, flood or war. Someone like Al Gore needs to have the courage to stand up and exhort Americans to eat less meat so that others do not go hungry.

New Generations of Biofuels

But here's the point about biofuels that critics overlook: today's biofuels are a transitional form of liquid fuel, and by setting standards for a new generation of biofuels, we can reap their benefits without harmful environmental side effects. Backers of corn ethanol do their best to point out its positives: it is replacing imported petroleum and its use in gasoline as an oxygenator does make gasoline less polluting. (MTBE, the chemical it replaced, had to be phased out because it seeks out and pollutes underground water supplies.) But after much expert analysis of the life cycle benefits and drawbacks, it's clear that corn ethanol, especially when made with energy from coal, has a negative impact on the environment.

However, change is on the way. Visible in a story here and there is the reality that we are in the midst of an explosion of entrepreneurial effort and progress toward commercialization of an improved generation of biofuels. An array of new companies are using and commercializing biofuel production from waste products or non-food vegetation like switchgrass. Thanks to the inconsistent policies and pro-oil bias of Congress and various presidents, we are years behind where we should be in this development, but progress now seems irreversible. For example, Range Fuels of Broomfield, Colorado, plans to make ethanol from slash, the bark and branches left over from the harvesting of pines grown on plantations. Range recently raised $100 million to complete a facility next year in Soperton, Georgia, that it says will be able to make 20 million gallons of ethanol a year from slash.

An even better fuel source may turn out to be green algae, the stuff that grows in virtually any pool of stagnant water (it need not be of drinking quality) and that is exposed to sunlight. Fortunately, algae feed on carbon dioxide and grow very fast. The possibilities are tantalizing. For example, Greenfuels Technology of Cambridge, Massachusetts, is currently scaling up an algae farm at a power plant in Arizona. The carbon dioxide emitted by the power plant is fed to the algae, which are then harvested to make either ethanol or biodiesel. If this process is successful on a large scale, it opens up the possibility of recycling power-plant CO2 emissions to create abundant liquid fuel to replace petroleum. That would be a Holy Grail indeed.

A New Direction

It is not an exaggeration to say that entrepreneurs are in a race to successfully commercialize the next generation of biofuels. Backing for these efforts is coming from venture capitalists and companies like Waste Management, the behemoth of the garbage industry; the Royal Dutch Shell Group; E.I. Dupont De Nemours; Goldman Sachs; and Khosla Ventures, a venture capital firm run by Vinod Khosla, a founder of Sun Microsystems. If the maxim of following the money is any guide, then the road to viable, sustainable biofuels is under construction.

The market forces already in play can be shoved in the right direction—and, of course, the wrong one—with government mandates and standards. Minnesota, for example, has mandated for several years now that all diesel fuel sold there must contain 2 percent biodiesel, and is raising the requirement to 5 percent. The reason is that gallon for gallon, soybean biodiesel lowers CO emissions by 78 percent, compared to petroleum diesel, according to the latest estimate, and dramatically lowers emissions of the tiny particulates implicated in asthma. But America's biodiesel industry is currently in a faint, operating at only about 20 percent capacity, and exporting to Europe much of what it is making. A major reason for this is that the infrastructure to blend biodiesel into petroleum diesel is lacking. Nationally, trucks that supply retail outlets with gasoline and diesel pick it up at 1,500 terminals. Only forty-two of them, less than 3 percent, are equipped to handle biodiesel, with many of those located in or near Minnesota. So even though the industry has the capacity to send 2.21 billion gallons of biodiesel to market, according to the best estimate of the National Biodiesel Board, a trade group, we are, instead, still burning 80 percent of that amount in the form of polluting petroleum diesel. This is particularly harmful in inner cities, where pollution from diesel buses and trucks is concentrated. But without assured demand for biodiesel, terminal operators are unwilling to invest the $1.5 million necessary to construct necessary special facilities at each terminal.

It is not an exaggeration to say that entrepreneurs are in a race to successfully commercialize the next generation of biofuels.

The Politics of Biofuels

Biodiesel proponents expect the industry to recover next year when new federal requirements for use of alternative fuels go into effect, including a specific requirement for use of 500 million gallons of biodiesel. But here is where the fight is taking place over ethanol. While the Energy Independence and Security Act of 2007 mandates steadily increasing use of both biodiesel and next generation ethanol it also guarantees the continued existence of the corn ethanol industry. In fact, it ratchets up the required use of corn ethanol from 10.5 billion gallons in 2009 to 15 billion by 2015. As is the way inside the Beltway, the legislation thus satisfied the political needs of members of Congress from corn-growing states. Given the unintended consequences of pushing up corn ethanol production so rapidly, Congress needs to revisit those targets and to do it quickly, in fairness to farmers who need time and consistent policy to manage their farms effectively. Sophisticated studies published early this year [2008] show clearly that whether biofuels reduce carbon dioxide emissions depends on where and how they are produced.

A Better Way

However, there may be a better approach that gets politicians out of the business of micromanaging production of food crops. Some environmental scientists, like the late Alex Farrell of the University of California at Berkeley, have advised against setting specific targets by fuel type. Instead, they favor an approach that has been adopted in California. In January, 2007, Governor Arnold Schwarzenegger signed an executive order mandating that by 2020 the carbon content of any and all passenger vehicle fuel sold in the state—including petroleum—be reduced from current levels by 10 percent, a preliminary goal. How fuel suppliers make that cut will be up to them. They can get there by mixing a cleaner fuel into gasoline, for example, or by buying and trading carbon credits.

Because Californians use about 11 percent of all the gasoline consumed in the United States, the order is expected to have substantial impact.

Biofuel production is not the silver bullet for global warming, but it can be part of the solution.

A Big Challenge

More comprehensive standards on an international level are also in the works. A draft of an international rating system for biofuels may be ready early in 2009. It could result in a labeling system that takes into account the impact of fuels not only on the environment but also on social justice concerns including food security and workers' rights. "Many people are worried about biofuels contributing to deforestation and air pollution in the name of protecting the planet," said Claude Martin, member of the board of the International Institute for Sustainable Development and chair of the steering committee of the Roundtable on Sustainable Biofuels. The roundtable, whose headquarters are at the University of Lausanne, Switzerland, has been holding a series of meetings that include manufacturers, conservation leaders, government and UN representatives and non-governmental organizations. "The roundtable will bring together all these actors . . . to ensure that biofuels deliver on their promise of sustainability," he said.

That is unquestionably a tall order. But so is every aspect of the revolution necessary to end the era of fossil fuels. Biofuel production is not the silver bullet for global warming, but it can be part of the solution. Generating electric power entirely from solar, wind and geothermal by the end of 2018, as Al Gore has boldly proposed, would be another big piece. But there's also a need to break the silence around the role of American eating habits in global warming and global hunger. Reducing our addiction to meat may not be popular, but we need to view our love affair with burgers and barbecue in the same frame as gas-guzzling SUVs.

3

Biofuels Are Bad for Feeding People and Combating Climate Change

David Biello

David Biello is a contributor to Scientific American.

Two studies from 2008 show that converting corn to ethanol not only leads to more clearing of the Amazon rainforest, but can exacerbate the problem of climate change. It also drives up food prices, causing food shortages and increased hunger and malnutrition in poor countries. Although there are benefits to producing and consuming biofuels, the energy industry and the US government must be careful to pursue biofuel research and development that will not increase climate change.

Converting corn to ethanol in Iowa not only leads to clearing more of the Amazonian rainforest, researchers report in a pair of new studies in *Science*, but also would do little to slow global warming—and often make it worse.

"Prior analyses made an accounting error," says one study's lead author, Tim Searchinger, an agricultural expert at Princeton University. "There is a huge imbalance between the carbon lost by plowing up a hectare [2.47 acres] of forest or grassland from the benefit you get from biofuels."

Growing plants store carbon in their roots, shoots and leaves. As a result, the world's plants and the soil in which they grow contain nearly three times as much carbon as the entire atmosphere. "I know when I look at a tree that half the dry weight of it is carbon," says ecologist David Tilman of the University of Minnesota, coauthor of the other study which examined the "carbon debt" embedded in any biofuel. "That's going to end up as carbon dioxide in the atmosphere when you cut it down."

By turning crops such as corn, sugarcane and palm oil into biofuels—whether ethanol, biodiesel, or something else— proponents hope to reap the benefits of the carbon soaked up as the plants grow to offset the carbon dioxide (CO_2) emitted when the resulting fuel is burned. But whether biofuels emit more or less CO_2 than gasoline depends on what the land they were grown on was previously used for, both studies show.

Tilman and his colleagues examined the overall CO_2 released when land use changes occur. Converting the grasslands of the U.S. to grow corn results in excess greenhouse gas emissions of 134 metric tons of CO_2 per hectare—a debt that would take 93 years to repay by replacing gasoline with corn-based ethanol. And converting jungles to palm plantations or tropical rainforest to soy fields would take centuries to pay back their carbon debts. "Any biofuel that causes land clearing is likely to increase global warming," says ecologist Joseph Fargione of The Nature Conservancy, lead author of the second study. "It takes decades to centuries to repay the carbon debt that is created from clearing land."

Turning food into fuel also has the unintended consequence of driving up food prices, reducing the access of the neediest populations to grains and meat.

Diverting food crops into fuel production leads to ever more land clearing as well. Ethanol demand in the U.S., for example, has caused some farmers to plant more corn and less soy. This has driven up soy prices causing farmers in Brazil to clear more Amazon rainforest land to plant valuable soy, Searchinger's study notes. Because a soy field contains far less carbon than a rainforest, the greenhouse gas benefit of the original ethanol is wiped out. "Corn-based ethanol, instead of producing a 20 percent savings [in greenhouse gas emissions], nearly doubles greenhouse emissions over 30 years and increases greenhouse gases for 167 years," the researchers write. "We can't get to a result with corn ethanol where we can generate greenhouse gas benefits," Searchinger adds.

Turning food into fuel also has the unintended consequence of driving up food prices, reducing the access of the neediest populations to grains and meat. "It's equivalent to saying we will try to reduce greenhouse gases by reducing food consumption," Searchinger says. "Unfortunately, a lot of that comes from the world's poorest people."

"We are converting their food into our fuel," Tilman notes. "The typical driver of an SUV spends as much on fuel in a month as the poorer third of the world spend on food."

The studies do find some benefit from biofuels but only when planted on agricultural land too dry or degraded for food production or significant tree or plant growth and only when derived from native plants, such as a mix of prairie grasses in the U.S. Midwest. Or such fuels can be made from waste: corn stalks, leftover wood from timber production or even city garbage.

But that will not slake a significant portion of the growing thirst for transportation fuels. "If we convert every corn kernel grown today in the U.S. to ethanol we offset just 12 percent of our gasoline use," notes ecologist Jason Hill of the University of Minnesota. "The real benefit to these advanced biofuels may not be in displacement of fossil fuels but in the building up of carbon stores in the soil."

Of course, there is another reason for biofuels: energy independence. "Biofuels like ethanol are the only tool readily available that can begin to address the challenge of energy security," Bob Dinneen, president of industry group the Renewable Fuels Association said in a statement. "The alternative is to continue to exploit increasingly costlier fossil fuels for which the environmental price tag will be great."

But the environmental price tag of biofuels now joins the ranks of other, cheaper domestic fuel sources—such as coal-to-liquid fuel—as major sources of globe-warming pollution as well as unintended social consequences. As a result, 10 prominent scientists have written a letter to President Bush and other government leaders urging them to "shape policies to assure that government incentives for biofuels do not increase global warming."

"We shouldn't abandon biofuels," Searchinger says. But "you don't solve global warming by going in the wrong direction."

4

Biofuels May Have a Promising Future

Economist

The Economist *is a news magazine based in the United Kingdom.*

New technologies have renewed hopes that biofuels will replace fossil fuels and allow the United States to become energy independent. One area that has made considerable progress is the cellulosic ethanol industry. Another is biodiesels, which are more easily produced and have a larger potential market. Technology is being developed to mass produce biodiesel from algae, which is the most intriguing of all the new technologies and may be the biofuel of the future.

Make something people want to buy at a price they can afford. Hardly a revolutionary business strategy, but one that the American biofuels industry has, to date, eschewed. Now a new wave of companies think that they have the technology to change the game and make unsubsidised profits. If they can do so reliably, and on a large scale, biofuels may have a lot more success in freeing the world from fossil fuels than they have had until now.

The original 1970s appeal of biofuels was the opportunity to stick up a finger or two, depending on the local bodily idiom, to the oil sheikhs. Over time, the opportunity to fight global warming added to the original energy-security appeal.

Make petrol out of plants in a sufficiently clever way and you can drive around with no net emissions of carbon dioxide as well as no net payments to the mad, the bad and the greedy. A great idea all round, then.

The Failure of Ethanol

Sadly, in America, it did not work out like that. First, the fuel was not petrol. Instead, it was ethanol, which stores less energy per litre, tends to absorb water and is corrosive; people will use it only if it is cheap or if you force them to through mandatory blending. In Brazil, which turned to biofuels after the 1970s oil shocks, the price of ethanol eventually became low enough for the fuel to find a market, thanks to highly productive sugar plantations and distilleries powered by the pulp left when that sugar was extracted from its cane. As a result Brazil is now a biofuels superpower. North American ethanol is mostly made from corn (maize), which is less efficient, and often produced in distilleries powered by coal; it is thus neither as cheap nor as environmentally benign. But American agribusiness, which knows a good thing when it sees one, used its political clout to arrange subsidies and tariffs that made corn-ethanol profitable and that kept out the alternative from Brazil.

The original 1970s appeal of biofuels was the opportunity to stick up a finger or two, depending on the local bodily idiom, to the oil sheikhs.

This still left the problem: using corn limits the size of the industry and pits it against the interests of people who want food. Boosters claimed that cellulose, from which the stalks, leaves and wood of plants are made, could if suitably treated become a substitute for the starch in corn. Both starch and cellulose consist of sugar molecules, linked together in different ways, and sugar is what fermentation feeds on. But cellulosic biofuel has so far failed, on an epic scale, to deliver. At the moment, only a handful of factories around the world produce biofuel from cellulose. And that fuel is still ethanol.

Drop-in Fuels

This is what companies working on a new generation of biofuels want to change. Instead of ethanol, they plan to make hydrocarbons, molecules chemically much more similar to those that already power planes, trains and automobiles. These will, they say, be "drop-in" fuels, any quantity of which can be put into the appropriate fuel tanks and pipelines with no fuss whatsoever. For that reason alone, they are worth more than ethanol.

Appropriately designed drop-in fuels can substitute for diesel and aviation fuel, which ethanol cannot. That increases the size of the potential market. They also have advantages on the production side. Because crude oils from different places have different chemical compositions, containing some molecules engines won't like, oil refineries today need to do a lot of careful tweaking. The same applies to the production of biodiesel from plant oils. Genetically engineered bugs making hydrocarbons more or less from scratch could guarantee consistent quality without the hassle, thus perhaps commanding a premium with no extra effort. Meanwhile the feedstock could be nice and cheap: Brazilian sugar. Tariffs that block Brazilian ethanol from northern markets do not apply to drop-in hydrocarbons.

Scale Models

If this approach works, it will not only be beneficial in its own right—modestly reducing greenhouse-gas emissions while making money for its investors—it will also provide a lasting market incentive to scientists to devise better ways of turning cellulose into sugar. This gives the prospects for this generation of biofuels a plausibility that was missing from its predecessors. The drop-in firms are starting to come out of the laboratory, float themselves on the stockmarket, team up with oil companies and build their first factories. The dice, in other words, are rolling.

One of the leaders of the drop-in drive is Alan Shaw, the boss of Codexis, a firm based in Redwood City, California, which makes specialised enzymes that perform tricky chemical conversions. In Dr Shaw's opinion, the industry's problem has not been bad products so much as a failure to think big.

Dr Shaw proposes to remedy that. In collaboration with Shell, an Anglo-Dutch oil company, and Cosan, Brazil's third-largest sugar producer, he plans to build a factory capable of producing 400m litres (2.5m barrels, or 105m gallons) of drop-in fuel every year. The other companies will provide money, reaction vessels and sugar. He will provide the enzymes and genetically engineered bacteria needed to make a drop-in fuel.

The drop-in firms are starting to come out of the laboratory, float themselves on the stock market, team up with oil companies and build their first factories.

The project is part of a joint venture by Shell and Cosan; with a capacity of more than 2 billion litres a year, it is the world's largest biofuel operation, and it owns a 16.4% stake in Codexis. At the moment, the joint venture's business is based on fermenting cane sugar into ethanol, but the new plant would start changing that. Codexis's enzymes and bacteria can turn sugar into molecules called straight-chain alkanes which have between 12 and 16 carbon atoms in them. Such alkanes are the main ingredients of diesel fuel.

Developing Drop-in Biodiesels

In April [2010] Codexis became the first start-up involved in drop-in fuels to float itself on a stockmarket—which in this case was NASDAQ, America's main market for high-tech stocks. But it is not the last. Another firm that recently completed its NASDAQ flotation is Amyris, of Emeryville, which is also in the San Francisco Bay area. Amyris started off using large-scale genetic engineering, also known as synthetic biology, to create bugs that make a malaria drug. But now it, too, has a product that it claims is a drop-in biodiesel. And it, too, has hooked up with an oil company: Total, of France, which owns 17% of the firm.

Amyris's biodiesel is made of more complicated molecules than Codexis's (they are known, technically, as terpenes), and the firm employs genetically engineered yeast, rather than bacteria. But Brazilian sugar is again used as the raw material. Amyris has formed a joint venture with Santelisa Vale, Brazil's second-largest sugar company, and is busy refitting some of that firm's ethanol plants in order to make drop-in diesel.

The Codexis-Cosan-Shell partnership and the Amyris-Santelisa-Total one are the furthest along of the drop-in fuel businesses, but others are coming up on the rails. LS9, which is based in South San Francisco (a separate municipality that has a cluster of biotech companies), also uses bacteria to make straight-chain alkanes. It is converting a fermentation plant in Florida into a test facility to see if what works in the laboratory will work at scale. And Virent, based in Madison, Wisconsin, is making alkanes out of sugars using a chemical, rather than a biological, process.

Butanols

Gevo, of Englewood, Colorado, which filed for flotation on NASDAQ in August [2010], is planning to make another type of post-ethanol fuel: butanol. Like Codexis, it will use enzymes and genetically engineered bugs to do this; like Amyris and LS9, it will retrofit existing ethanol plants to keep the cost down. The aim is to turn out an annual 2 billion litres of butanol by 2014. BP, a British petroleum company, is building a butanol pilot plant to do this near Hull in the north of England and also has big ambitions for the fuel.

Like ethanol, butanol is an alcohol. That means each of its molecules contains an oxygen atom as well as the carbon and hydrogen found in an alkane. Butanol, however, has four carbon atoms in its molecules, whereas ethanol has two. That gives butanol more energy for a given mass and makes it more alkane-like in its properties; nor does it absorb water as readily as ethanol. Moreover, the production process for butanol is more efficient than the processes that produce alkanes; proportionately more of the energy from the feedstock (various crops for Gevo, wheat for BP) ends up in the final fuel. And BP will certainly be able to bring to the party the ambitious scale that Dr Shaw praises.

[I]f drop-in fuels are to become a truly big business they need a wider range of feedstocks.

The Potential of Algae

The last of the Bay-area drop-in contenders is, in many ways, the most intriguing. Solazyme, another firm based in South San Francisco, wants to use single-celled algae to make its fuel. This is not a new idea. Craig Venter, who led the privately financed version of the Human Genome Project, is trying it too, through his latest venture, Synthetic Genomics, in San Diego. Synthetic Genomics is backed by the biggest oil beast of them all, ExxonMobil—and several other firms have similar ideas, if not the same heavyweight backing. Solazyme's approach is unusual, though. Instead of growing its algae in sunlit ponds it keeps them in the dark and feeds them with sugar.

At first sight this seems bonkers. The attraction of algae would seem to lie in the possibility that, since they photosynthesise, they could be engineered to contain the whole sunlight-to-fuel process in one genetically engineered package. Sunshine being free, this looked a brilliant idea. But looks can be deceptive. If you keep your algae in ponds the rays do not always strike them at the best angle and the algae sometimes shade one another if they are growing densely. Photobioreactors—complicated systems of transparent piping through which alga-rich water is pumped—overcome those problems, but they cost a lot and are hard to keep clean. Solazyme tried both of these approaches, and almost went bankrupt in the process. Then its founders, Jonathan Wolfson and Harrison Dillon, asked themselves whether it might not be cheaper to ignore the photosynthetic step, buy the sugar that photosynthesis produces instead, and concentrate on getting the algae to turn it into oil.

Which is what the firm now does. It also has a nice little earner in the form of a contract with the American navy. The navy intends that, by 2020, half the fuel it uses (over six billion litres a year, mainly diesel and jet fuel) will be from renewable sources. Over the past year Solazyme has been providing it with trial quantities of both from its production facilities in Pennsylvania and Iowa. The algal oils are not themselves good fuel; but a refinery in Houston takes care of that, producing shipshape alkanes of the sort the navy likes.

High-fiber Diet

The success of all this obviously depends on the price of sugar, which is rising. Historically, the cost of making Brazilian ethanol has been about 26 cents a litre. Diesel will cost more, but petroleum-based diesel sells in America for 57 cents a litre before distribution costs and tax, so there should be room for profit. Nevertheless, if drop-in fuels are to become a truly big business they need a wider range of feedstocks.

Until recently, the assumption has been that cellulose would take over from sugar and starch as the feedstock for making biofuels. Making cellulose into sugar is technically possible, and many firms are working on that possibility. Some are using enzymes. Some are using micro-organisms. Still others have a hybrid approach, part biotechnological and part traditional chemistry. And some go for pure chemistry, breaking the cellulose down into a gaseous mixture of hydrogen and carbon monoxide before building it back up into something more useful.

The reason for this enthusiasm has been government mandates: America's Renewable Fuel Standard (RFS-2) and its European equivalent. On pain of fines, but with the carrot of subsidies, these require that a certain amount of renewable fuel be blended into petroleum-based fuels over the next decade or so. RFs-2 calls for a 10% blend of cellulosic fuel by 2022.

The targets in RFS-2, though, represent a huge climbdown. Its predecessor, RFS-1, called for 379m litres of cellulosic ethanol to be produced in 2010; RFS-2 mandates only 25m litres. The industry in fact has a capacity of about 70m litres today, according to the Biotechnology Industry Organisation (BIO), an American lobby group.

The Failed Potential of Cellulosic Ethanol

The reduced expectations reflect the fact that making fuel out of cellulose turns out to be hard and costly. Today's cellulosic ethanol is competitive with the petrol it is supposed to displace only when the price of crude oil reaches $120 a barrel. In Dr Shaw's view, a lot can be done by scaling up (and using the appropriate enzymes, of course, which Codexis will be only too happy to sell you). And big plants will, indeed, bring the price down—probably not to the point where cellulosic ethanol can compete in a fair fight, but quite possibly to a level at which fuel companies will make or buy the stuff rather than pay fines for not doing so.

Phil New, the head of biofuels at BP, says his firm is determined to comply with RFS-2. To that end it is planning a plant in Florida that will have a capacity of 137m litres when it comes on stream in 2013. It is one of seven cellulosic-ethanol fermentation plants with annual capacities above 38m litres (that is, 10m gallons) which BIO says should be running by 2013, with a further seven making ethanol using syngas conversion. However, such claims are not that different from those made three years ago—which singularly failed to bear fruit.

Grassed Up

If things work out better this time, it still leaves the question of where the cellulose is to come from. The answer is likely, in one form or another, to be grass.

Though they look very different, sugar cane and corn are both grasses. So is wheat, which is corn's counterpart as the starch source of choice in the EU [European Union]. A simple way of garnering cellulose is to gather up the leftovers when these crops have been processed—bagasse from sugar cane, stover from corn and straw from wheat.

That is a start, but it will not be enough, Wood is a possibility, particularly if it is dealt with chemically, rather than biologically (much of the carbon in wood is in the form of lignin, a molecule that is even tougher than cellulose). But energy-rich grasses look like the best bet. Ceres, which is based in Thousand Oaks, California, has taken several species of fast-growing grass, notably switchgrass and sorghum, and supercharged them to grow even faster and put on more weight by using a mixture of selective breeding and genetic engineering. Part of America's prairies, the firm hopes, will revert to grassland and provide the cellulose that biofuels will need. The Energy Biosciences Institute that BP is funding at the University of Illinois, in Urbana-Champaign, is working on hybrid miscanthus, an ornamental grass that can produce truly remarkable yields.

Room for Improvement

If the price were right, such energy crops might take America a fair bit of the way to the "energy independence" that early proselytisers for biofuels crowed about. A study carried out last year [2009] by Sandia National Laboratories, an American government outfit, suggests that in theory 285 billion litres of cellulosic biofuel a year could be extracted from the country's agriculture and forestry without breaking too much sweat. That is 1.8 billion barrels, compared with American oil imports of 4.3 billion barrels in 2009. Europe's higher human-population density leaves less space for energy crops. But there is clearly some room for expansion in the Old World as well as the New.

Beyond the rich countries, capacity is greater still. In a fit of enthusiasm a few years ago Steven Chu, now America's energy secretary, floated the idea of a global glucose economy to replace oil. That is going a bit far. Brazil is a well-governed country, but other parts of the tropics, though endowed with sunshine and cheap land, are not always the sorts of places that the wise investor would pile into. And Brazil's blessings in terms of oodles of land that can grow cane with no irrigation are not widespread. Nevertheless, the country's success shows that international trade in biofuels is a possibility. If it brought economic development to less favoured lands, that would surely be welcome.

Over the long run, the future for biofuels may be looking up.

Drop in or Drop out

Such a future, though, depends on cars continuing to be powered by liquid fuels. A large shift to electric cars would put the kibosh on the biofuel market as currently conceived by most of its supporters; but it would not necessarily kill the principle of using plants to convert sunlight into car-power. The goal of reducing emissions needs low-carbon generators to power the grid the electric cars draw juice from. Put the energy crops in generators instead of distilleries and off you go.

Richard Hamilton, the boss of Ceres, says he is indifferent as to whether his grasses end up in petrol tanks or power stations. Others think making them into electricity might be a better answer anyway. A study published last year [2009] by Elliott Campbell, of the University of California, Merced, and his colleagues suggested that turning crops into electricity, not fuel, would propel America's cars 80% farther and reduce greenhouse-gas emissions even more. Electrons are easy to transport and burning uses all of the fuel value of a plant—including that stored in the lignin which current processing methods find hard to deal with.

The electrification of cars, however the electricity might be generated, would be the end of the road for ethanol. But not necessarily for drop-ins. There is no realistic prospect for widespread electric air travel: the jet engines on aircraft need the high-energy density that only chemical fuels can provide. So if you want low-carbon flying, drop-in biofuels are the only game in town. And civil aviation alone is expected to use 250 billion litres of fuel this year [2010], is growing fast and could pay a premium if its emissions were subject to a cap or a tax. Over the long run, the future for biofuels may be looking up.

5

Biodiesel Should Not Be the Biofuel of the Future

George Monbiot

George Monbiot is an author and environmental and political activist.

Most of the biodiesel being produced in the world is made from palm oil, because it is cheaper than biodiesel made from any other crops. The increasing demand for biodiesel has led to horrible deforestation in many countries, as forests are converted to palm farms. As swamp forests are being cleared, the exposed peat dries and releases large amounts of carbon dioxide into the atmosphere. The whole process is an environmental disaster. Instead of subsidizing failed biofuels like biodiesel, governments should be focusing on cutting back on fuel consumption.

Over the past two years [2003 to 2005] I have made an uncomfortable discovery. Like most environmentalists, I have been as blind to the constraints affecting our energy supply as my opponents have been to climate change. I now realise that I have entertained a belief in magic.

Facing the Facts

In 2003, the biologist Jeffrey Dukes calculated that the fossil fuels we burn in one year were made from organic matter "containing 44 x 1018 grams of carbon, which is more than 400 times the net primary productivity of the planet's current biota". In plain English, this means that every year we use four centuries' worth of plants and animals.

The idea that we can simply replace this fossil legacy—and the extraordinary power densities it gives us—with ambient energy is the stuff of science fiction. There is simply no substitute for cutting back. But substitutes are being sought everywhere. They are being promoted today at the climate talks in Montreal, by states—such as ours—that seek to avoid the hard decisions climate change demands. And at least one substitute is worse than the fossil-fuel burning it replaces.

Underestimating the Destructive Qualities of Biodiesel

The last time I drew attention to the hazards of making diesel fuel from vegetable oils, I received as much abuse as I have ever been sent for my stance on the Iraq war. The biodiesel missionaries, I discovered, are as vociferous in their denial as the executives of Exxon. I am now prepared to admit that my previous column was wrong. But they're not going to like it. I was wrong because I underestimated the fuel's destructive impact.

Before I go any further, I should make it clear that turning used chip fat into motor fuel is a good thing. The people slithering around all day in vats of filth are performing a service to society. But there is enough waste cooking oil in the UK to meet a 380th of our demand for road transport fuel. Beyond that, the trouble begins.

[T]he biodiesel missionaries, I discovered, are as vociferous in their denial as the executives of Exxon.

When I wrote about it last year [2004], I thought that the biggest problem caused by biodiesel was that it set up a competition for land use. Arable land that would otherwise have been used to grow food would instead be used to grow fuel.

But now I find that something even worse is happening. The biodiesel industry has accidentally invented the world's most carbon-intensive fuel.

The Most Destructive Crop on Earth

In promoting biodiesel—as the EU [European Union], the British and US governments and thousands of environmental campaigners do—you might imagine that you are creating a market for old chip fat, or rapeseed oil, or oil from algae grown in desert ponds. In reality you are creating a market for the most destructive crop on earth.

Last week [November, 2005], the chairman of Malaysia's federal land development authority announced that he was about to build a new biodiesel plant. His was the ninth such decision in four months. Four new refineries are being built in Peninsula Malaysia, one in Sarawak and two in Rotterdam. Two foreign consortiums—one German, one American—are setting up rival plants in Singapore. All of them will be making biodiesel from the same source: oil from palm trees.

"The demand for biodiesel," the Malaysian Star reports, "will come from the European Community . . . This fresh demand . . . would, at the very least, take up most of Malaysia's crude palm oil inventories." Why? Because it is cheaper than biodiesel made from any other crop.

The Environmental Impact of Palm-Oil Use

In September [2005], Friends of the Earth published a report about the impact of palm oil production. "Between 1985 and 2000," it found, "the development of oil-palm plantations was responsible for an estimated 87 per cent of deforestation in Malaysia". In Sumatra and Borneo, some 4 million hectares of forest have been converted to palm farms. Now a further 6 million hectares are scheduled for clearance in Malaysia, and 16.5 million in Indonesia.

Almost all the remaining forest is at risk. Even the famous Tanjung Puting national park in Kalimantan is being ripped apart by oil planters. The orangutan is likely to become extinct in the wild. Sumatran rhinos, tigers, gibbons, tapirs, proboscis monkeys and thousands of other species could go the same way. Thousands of indigenous people have been evicted from their lands, and some 500 Indonesians have been tortured when they tried to resist. The forest fires which every so often smother the region in smog are mostly started by the palm growers. The entire region is being turned into a gigantic vegetable oil field.

Before oil palms, which are small and scrubby, are planted, vast forest trees, containing a much greater store of carbon, must be felled and burnt. Having used up the drier lands, the plantations are moving into the swamp forests, which grow on peat. When they've cut the trees, the planters drain the ground. As the peat dries it oxidises, releasing even more carbon dioxide than the trees. In terms of its impact on both the local and global environments, palm biodiesel is more destructive than crude oil from Nigeria.

[K]nowing that they will accelerate rather than ameliorate climate change, the government has decided to go ahead anyway.

A Failure of Political Will

The British government understands this. In a report published last month [November, 2005], when it announced that it would obey the EU and ensure that 5.75% of our transport fuel came from plants by 2010, it admitted "the main environmental risks are likely to be those concerning any large expansion in biofuel feedstock production, and particularly in Brazil (for sugar cane) and south-east Asia (for palm oil plantations)."

It suggested that the best means of dealing with the problem was to prevent environmentally destructive fuels from being imported. The government asked its consultants whether a ban would infringe world trade rules. The answer was yes: "Mandatory environmental criteria ... would greatly increase the risk of international legal challenge to the policy as a whole." So it dropped the idea of banning imports, and called for "some form of voluntary scheme" instead. Knowing that the creation of this market will lead to a massive surge in imports of palm oil, knowing that there is nothing meaningful it can do to prevent them, and knowing that they will accelerate rather than ameliorate climate change, the government has decided to go ahead anyway.

At other times it happily defies the EU. But what the EU wants and what the government wants are the same. "It is essential that we balance the increasing demand for travel," the government's report says, "with our goals for protecting the environment." Until recently, we had a policy of reducing the demand for travel. Now, though no announcement has been made, that policy has gone. Like the Tories in the early 1990s, the Labour administration seeks to accommodate demand, however high it rises.... Instead of attempting to reduce demand, it is trying to alter supply. It is prepared to sacrifice the south-east Asian rainforests in order to be seen to be doing something, and to allow motorists to feel better about themselves.

All this illustrates the futility of the technofixes now being pursued in Montreal. Trying to meet a rising demand for fuel is madness, wherever the fuel might come from. The hard decisions have been avoided, and another portion of the biosphere is going up in smoke.

6

Cellulosic Ethanol
Shows Promise

Evan Ratliff

Evan Ratliff is a contributing editor at Wired.

Cellulosic ethanol shows potential as an alternative fuel source, but so far scientists have struggled to make it affordable. Part of the reason is the chemistry: cellulose is a tough molecule to break down, especially in a cost-effective manner. There has been a flood of research and funding into cellulosic ethanol in recent years, and hopes run high that the technology can be developed to the point it becomes an economically attractive alternative to corn ethanol and other biofuels.

On a blackboard, it looks so simple: Take a plant and extract the cellulose. Add some enzymes and convert the cellulose molecules into sugars. Ferment the sugar into alcohol. Then distill the alcohol into fuel. One, two, three, four—and we're powering our cars with lawn cuttings, wood chips, and prairie grasses instead of Middle East oil.

The Economics

Unfortunately, passing chemistry class doesn't mean acing economics. Scientists have long known how to turn trees into ethanol, but doing it profitably is another matter. We can run our cars on lawn cuttings today; we just can't do it at a price people are willing to pay.

The problem is cellulose. Found in plant cell walls, it's the most abundant naturally occurring organic molecule on the planet, a potentially limitless source of energy. But it's a tough molecule to break down. Bacteria and other microorganisms use specialized enzymes to do the job, scouring lawns, fields and forest floors, hunting out cellulose and dining on it. Evolution has given other animals elegant ways to do the same: Cows, goats, and deer maintain a special stomach full of bugs to digest the molecule; termites harbor hundreds of unique microorganisms in their guts that help them process it. For scientists, though, figuring out how to convert cellulose into a usable form on a budget driven by gas-pump prices has been neither elegant nor easy. To tap that potential energy, they're harnessing nature's tools, tweaking them in the lab to make them work much faster than nature intended.

Scientists have long known how to turn trees into ethanol, but doing it profitably is another matter.

While researchers work to bring down the costs of alternative energy sources, in the past two years [2005–2007] policymakers have finally reached consensus that it's time to move past oil. The reasoning varies—reducing our dependence on unstable oil-producing regions, cutting greenhouse gases, avoiding ever-increasing prices—but it's clear that the US needs to replace billions of gallons of gasoline with alternative fuels, and fast. Even oil industry veteran George W. Bush has declared that "America is addicted to oil" and set a target of replacing 20 percent of the nation's annual gasoline consumption—35 billion gallons—with renewable fuels by 2017.

Finding the Best Alternative

But how? Hydrogen is too far-out, and it's no easy task to power our cars with wind- or solar-generated electricity. The answer, then, is ethanol. Unfortunately, the ethanol we can make today—from corn kernels—is a mediocre fuel source. Corn ethanol is easier to produce than the cellulosic kind (convert the sugar to alcohol and you're basically done), but it generates at best 30 percent more energy than is required to grow and process the corn—hardly worth the trouble. Plus, crop's fertilizer-intensive cultivation pollutes waterways, and increased demand drives up food costs (corn prices doubled last year). And anyway, the corn ethanol industry is projected to produce, at most, the equivalent of only 15 billion gallons of fuel by 2017. "We can't make 35 billion gallons' worth of gasoline out of ethanol from corn," says Dartmouth engineering and biology professor Lee Lynd, "and we probably don't want to."

Cellulosic ethanol, in theory, is a much better bet. Most of the plant species suitable for producing this kind of ethanol—like switchgrass, a fast-growing plant found throughout the Great Plains, and farmed poplar trees—aren't food crops. And according to a joint study by the US Departments of Agriculture and Energy, we can sustainably grow more than 1 billions tons of such biomass on available farmland, using minimal fertilizer. In fact, about two-thirds of what we throw into our landfills today contains cellulose and thus potential fuel. Better still: Cellulosic ethanol yields roughly 80 percent more energy than is required to grow and convert it.

So a wave of public and private funding, bringing new-found optimism, is pouring into research labs. Venture capitalists have invested hundreds of millions of dollars in cellulosic-technology startups. BP [British Petroleum] has announced that it's giving $500 million for an Energy Biosciences Institute run by the University of Illinois and UC Berkeley. The Department of Energy [DOE] pledged $385 million to six companies building cellulosic demonstration plants. In June [2007] the DOE added awards for three $125 million bioenergy centers to pursue new research on cellulosic biofuels.

There's just one catch: No one has yet figured out how to generate energy from plant matter at a competitive price. The result is that no car on the road today uses a drop of cellulosic ethanol.

An Intractable Problem

Cellulose is a tough molecule by design, a fact that dates back 400 million years to when plants made the move from ocean to land and required sturdy cell walls to keep themselves upright and protected against microbes, the elements, and eventually animals. Turning that defensive armor into fuel involves pretreating the plant material with chemicals to strip off cell-wall protections. Then there are two complicated steps: first, introducing enzymes, called cellulases, to break the cellulose down into glucose and xylose; and second, using yeast and other microorganisms to ferment those sugars into ethanol.

The step that has perplexed scientists is the one involving enzymes—proteins that come in an almost infinite variety of three-dimensional structures. They are at work everywhere in living cells, usually speeding up the chemical reactions that break down complex molecules. Because they're hard to make from scratch, scientists generally extract them from microorganisms that produce them naturally. But the trick is producing the enzymes cheaply enough at an industrial scale and speed.

Today's cellulases are the enzyme equivalent of vacuum tubes: clunky, slow, and expensive. Now, flush with cash, scientists and companies are racing to develop the cellulosic transistor. Some researchers are trying to build the ultimate microbe in the lab, one that could combine the two key steps of the process. Others are using "directed evolution" and genetic engineering to improve the enzyme-producing microorganisms currently in use. Still others are combing the globe in search of new and better bugs. It's bio-construction versus bio-tinkering versus bio-prospecting, all with the single goal of creating the perfect enzyme cocktail.

President Bush, for one, seems to believe that the revolution is imminent. "It's an interesting time, isn't it," he mused this February [2007]. "We're on the verge of some break-throughs that will enable a pile of wood chips to become the raw materials for fuels that will run your car." Whether the car of the future will be powered by wood chips isn't clear yet. But it may depend on the success of the hunt for tiny enzymes that could be discovered anywhere from a termite's stomach in Central America to a lab bench to your own backyard.

The problem comes from the quotidian difficulties of making benchtop science work on an industrial scale.

The Forecast

Skeptics argue that rosy projections for cellulosic ethanol ignore its drawbacks—mainly, that cars need to be converted to run on it, that existing oil pipelines can't transport it, and that we don't have the land to grow enough of it. Advocates counter that if the fuel is cheap and plentiful enough, the infrastructure will follow. "If we could make ethanol at a large scale in a way that is sustainable, carbon-neutral, and cost-effective, we would surely be doing so," Lynd says, citing the fact that most cars can easily be converted to run on ethanol, something already done with most new cars in Brazil. "Meeting these objectives is not limited by the fuel properties of ethanol but rather by the current difficulty of converting cellulosic biomass to sugars."

Neither government funding nor venture capital, of course, guarantees research breakthroughs or commercial blockbusters. And even ardent proponents concede that cellulosic ethanol won't solve our fuel problems—or do much to stop global warming—without parallel efforts to improve vehicle efficiency. They also worry that attention could again fade if the first demonstration plants fail or oil prices plummet. "To get this industry going, you need some short-term breakthroughs, by which I mean the next five to seven years," says Martin Keller, a micro biologist at Oak Ridge National Laboratory in Tennessee and director of its new BioEnergy Science Center. "Otherwise, my fear is that people may leave this field again."

The problem comes from the quotidian difficulties of making benchtop science work on an industrial scale. Undoubtedly, even some well-funded efforts will fail. But the proliferation of research—the prospect of Lee Lynd's superbug, the evolution of current cellulases, and the addition of new enzymes harvested from nature—stacks the deck in favor of cellulosic ethanol.

No Silver Bullet

Alexander Karsner, assistant secretary for the DOE's Office of Energy Efficiency and Renewable Energy, says that with plants going up around the country, the industry could make cellulosic ethanol cost-competitive within six years. "I think there won't be a silver-bullet process, where you say, 'That has won, and everything else is done,'" he says. "So you need many of these technologies."

Having known lean times, Lynd is reluctant to predict the future. But given the freedom of fat wallets, he says, "I truly think that in five years all the hard issues about converting cellulosic biomass to ethanol may be solved."

The researchers' vision, of green and gold switchgrass fields feeding a nationwide network of ethanol plants and filling stations, often has an effortless quality to it—as easy as a few steps sketched out on a blackboard. The money and momentum is here. Solve the science, they argue, and the market will take care of the rest.

7

Corn Ethanol Is a Disaster

Cinnamon Stillwell

Cinnamon Stillwell is a journalist and political commentator.

The booming market for corn ethanol has resulted in higher food prices and food shortages, increased unemployment, and a potential water shortage. Environmentalists are concerned about other negative effects on the environment caused by the production of corn ethanol, particularly the destruction of the Amazon rainforest. In the US, politicians support corn ethanol as a way to garner support from voters in farming states. Government officials must approach the looming ethanol crisis carefully.

In the pantheon of well-intentioned governmental policies gone awry, massive ethanol biofuel production may go down as one of the biggest blunders in history. An unholy alliance of environmentalists, agribusiness, biofuel corporations and politicians has been touting ethanol as the cure to all our environmental ills, when in fact it may be doing more harm than good. An array of unintended consequences is wreaking havoc on the economy, food production and, perhaps most ironically, the environment.

What Are Biofuels?

Biofuels are fuels distilled from plant matter. Ethanol is corn-based, but other common biofuel sources include soybeans, sugar cane and palm oil, an edible vegetable oil. In the search for alternatives to fossil fuels, many countries have turned to biofuels, which has led to a booming business for those involved. In the United States, ethanol is the primary focus and, as a result, corn growers and ethanol producers are subsidized heavily by the government.

But it turns out that the use of food for fuel is wrought with difficulties. Corn, or some derivative thereof, is a common ingredient in a variety of packaged food products. So it's only natural that, as it becomes a rarer commodity due to the conflicting demands of biofuel production, the prices of those products will go up. The prices of food products containing barley and wheat are also on the rise as farmers switch to growing subsidized corn crops. During a time of economic instability, the last thing Americans need is higher prices at the grocery store, but that's exactly what they're getting.

At the same time, corn is the main ingredient in livestock feed and its dearth is causing prices of those products to rise as well. Farmers have had to scramble to find alternative sources of feed for their livestock and, in some cases, have had to sell off animals they can no longer afford to feed. This, in turn, has led to an increase in the price of meat and dairy products for consumers.

[T]he use of food for fuel is wrought with difficulties.

The Effect of Biofuels on the Economy

The hit on the livestock industry has also affected jobs, with countless employees being laid off due to the downturn. Pilgrim's Pride Corp., the nation's largest chicken producer, announced in March [2008] that it was closing a North Carolina chicken processing plant, and six of 13 U.S. distribution centers, due to the jump in feed costs. Even Iowa, the state that produces the most corn and therefore the supposed beneficiary of new jobs due to ethanol production, has seen its unemployment rate rise over the past year [2007]. The plant layoffs and closings already underway due to global competition and the fluctuating market have continued unabated.

Another adverse impact of ethanol production is potential water shortage. One gallon of ethanol requires four gallons of water to produce. According to a recent report from the National Research Council, an institution that focuses on science, engineering, technology and health, "increased production could greatly increase pressure on water supplies for drinking, industry, hydropower, fish habitat and recreation."

Not only is ethanol less productive than gasoline as a fuel source, its production is hurting the environment it was intended to preserve, particularly in the Third World. The amount of land needed to grow corn and other biofuel sources means that their production is leading to deforestation, the destruction of wetlands and grasslands, species extinction, displacement of indigenous peoples and small farmers, and loss of habitats that store carbon.

Biofuels Are a Disaster

Scientists predict that the Gulf of Mexico, already polluted by agricultural runoff from the United States, will only get worse as demand for ethanol, and therefore corn, increases. Meanwhile, rain forests throughout Central and South America are being razed to make way for land to grow biofuel components. Tortilla shortages in Mexico, rising flour prices in Pakistan, Indonesian and Malaysian forests being cut down and burned to make palm oil, and encroachments upon the Amazon rainforest due to Brazilian sugar cane production—all these developments indicate that biofuels are turning out to be more destructive than helpful.

The [March 27, 2008] issue of *Time* magazine addresses the subject in frightening detail. Michael Grunwald, author of the cover story, "The Clean Energy Scam," posits a worldwide epidemic that could end up being a greater disaster than all the alleged evils of fossil fuels combined. As he puts it:

"Deforestation accounts for 20 percent of all current carbon emissions. So unless the world can eliminate emissions from all other sources—cars, power plants, factories, even flatulent cows—it needs to reduce deforestation or risk an environmental catastrophe. That means limiting the expansion of agriculture, a daunting task as the world's population keeps expanding. And saving forests is probably an impossibility so long as vast expanses of cropland are used to grow modest amounts of fuel. The biofuels boom, in short, is one that could haunt the planet for generations—and it's only getting started."

"Insane" Policy

Accordingly, the United Nations has expressed skepticism about ethanol and other biofuels. But the European Union seems to have bought into the biofuel craze with proposed legislation to mandate its use. This proposal has set off alarm bells in the United Kingdom, particularly with the British government's chief science advisor, Professor John Beddington, who has warned that a food and deforestation crisis is likely to overtake any climate concerns. "The idea that you cut down rainforest to actually grow biofuels seems profoundly stupid," he stated. Similarly, the British government's top environmental scientist, Professor Robert Watson, called the policy "totally insane."

Some British environmentalists apparently agree, as do members of the American environmental movement. As noted in the aforementioned *Time* article, the Natural Resources Defense Council's Nathanael Greene, the author of a 2004 report that rallied fellow environmentalists to support biofuels, is "looking at the numbers in an entirely new way," now that biofuel production exists on such a large scale.

None of this has deterred American politicians from jumping on the ethanol bandwagon. No doubt, they see it as a means of garnering political support from the farm lobby and in particular ethanol producers, to whom they have provided generous federal subsidies. Indeed, President Bush, who according to his 2006 State of the Union address is a switchgrass enthusiast, has signed a bipartisan energy bill that will greatly increase support to the ethanol industry, as well as mandating the production of 36 billion gallons of biofuel by 2022.

While the search for alternatives to fossil fuels . . . is laudable, future avenues must be considered more carefully.

The Politics of Biofuels

In an election year, there has been no shortage of environmental platitudes aimed at voters and, inevitably, ethanol has been a mainstay. Democratic presidential candidate Hillary Clinton has been singing the praises of ethanol in Iowa, while her rival, Barack Obama, merely criticized her for not doing so earlier. Republican candidate John McCain, once an ardent opponent of ethanol, has suddenly become a convert.

The motto among both Democrats and Republicans on this issue seems to be "If it sounds good, push it," and a gullible public—seduced by climate change hysteria and a "Going Green!" advertising onslaught—is buying into it.

While the search for alternatives to fossil fuels, and in particular the dependence upon foreign sources thereof, is laudable, future avenues must be considered more carefully. As the looming ethanol disaster has demonstrated, yet again, the road to hell is paved with good intentions.

8

Corn Ethanol Is Not a Disaster

Kirk Leonard

Kirk Leonard is an author.

Corn ethanol has been a frequent target for critics of the biofuels industry. Most of the attacks are by critics associated with the oil and food industry. Many of the charges against corn ethanol are not backed up by scientific evidence. The fact is, corn ethanol is a vital piece in the world's energy transition from fossil fuels to clean alternative energy.

The first car Ferdinand Porsche built was electric. The first car Henry Ford built ran on ethanol. The first engine Rudolf Diesel built ran on peanut oil. With a century of petroleum experience behind us, we are getting back to basics. Electric cars and biofuels are coming back, thank goodness.

Biofuels as a Bridge

Biofuels provide a bridge and are a necessary piece of the energy transition we must do to sustain ourselves and our planet. Our agricultural and transportation systems depend on liquid fuels today. Smart land use decisions and good farming practices can provide both biofuels and sufficient food for all. Organic wastes will also become a significant biofuel feedstock.

Biofuels have been subject to more world media sustainability scrutiny than any "new" technology I am aware of, historically, which is both a good thing and unfortunate at the same time. A lot of good experience, data and direction have been gained and a lot of misinformation has been spread about biofuels.

The War on Corn Ethanol

Corn ethanol has been a particular target of naysayers. It has net negative greenhouse gas value! It causes deforestation, food shortages and price increases! It is net energy negative and causes engine problems! This is claptrap created by big businesses—big oil and big food in particular. Its purpose is to confuse people, and to support unsustainable, proprietary products and markets.

When has indirect land use change, a greenhouse gas (GHG) measure now being applied to biofuels, ever been considered in the development of an industry, for example? Has it ever been a consideration of leap-frog style urban expansion and its dramatic greenhouse gas effects—the loss of farm lands and carbon sequestration value, and increases in fossil fuel use? What about land despoiled by oil extraction, or lumber clear cuts? Is it fair, or even rational, to attribute all future land use changes to biofuels?

On GHG benefits, corn ethanol has shown impressive improvements since first being produced in volumes in the 1980's, and it has never been negative. A recent life-cycle analysis done for the International Energy Agency determined corn ethanol presents a substantial benefit, reducing GHGs, from "well to wheel" by 40% compared to gasoline, an appreciable amount, verifiable using current data and projected to increase to 55% by 2015.

Land Use Changes

On land use changes resulting from corn ethanol, there is no evidence of new US ag [agricultural] lands being used for corn cultivation, and there is no evidence of international land use changes, let alone deforestation, caused by corn ethanol. Normal farm crop decisions based on market factors have resulted in more US corn acreage, but other staple crops like soy and wheat are, like corn, in adequate supply and surplus. Another recent report concludes there is not likely to be any land use change associated with corn ethanol up to the maximum legislated amount of 15 billion gallons per year, set by Congress in 2007.

The ability to pay for or profit from food and weather remain the continuing primary sources of food access problems in the world. Corn ethanol and other biofuels have nothing to do with that. Food riots about rice costs have nothing to do with biofuels. Rice is not used for biofuel, and rice lands are not widely used for other biofuel crops.

The Economics of Corn Ethanol

Rational economic analyses of the impact of corn ethanol suggest a tiny effect—.2–3% of a family's food bill. A 2007 study concluded: "variations in the corn price 'explain' only 4% of the variations in the food CPI (Consumer Price Index). Thus, the corn price would be considered a statistically insignificant variable in determining what drives the food CPI." In light of normal inflation, continuing adequate supply and record surpluses, the food cost argument against ethanol is simply not valid.

Engines and Ethanol

One of the least rational but oft-cited issues with ethanol is engine problems. Since 1980, all engines sold in the US have been required to be ethanol compatible, so if you have experienced engine problems with ethanol blend fuels, something else is wrong. It isn't the ethanol.

A Reassessment of Ethanol

All this is not to say corn ethanol is good. It is not a good, long term biofuel solution, but in the US, it has paved the way. It is the principal oxygenate in gasoline today throughout the country. We have gained a great deal of experience in its development, and all of the facilities we have built will be equally useful with cellulosic ethanol, the next generation of bioethanol worldwide.

Biofuels are an essential piece of our energy future, as are greatly increased energy conservation and efficiency measures.

No less an authority than the US government has determined that biofuels made from food crops must be limited. They have put a limit on corn ethanol. The biofuels industry is similarly oriented, seeking a future not based on food crops and sensitive to the displacement of food resources and lands.

Biofuels are an essential piece of our energy future, as are greatly increased energy conservation and efficiency measures. Developed well, using wastes and non-food crops, focused on marginal or damaged lands, employing organic, low-input and no-till cropping practices, they can provide tremendous energy and environmental benefits.

9

The United States Is Resolute in Its Support for Ethanol

Timothy Gardner and Charles Abbott

Timothy Gardner is an energy and environment correspondent for Reuters. Charles Abbott is a journalist for Reuters.

Despite attacks on the growing ethanol industry, the US government remains steadfast in its support. Corn ethanol makes up a significant percentage of US energy consumption, and the next generation of biofuels are still being developed. Experts believe that changing energy policy would be too expensive and difficult—especially in a country with a political system that has shown little political will to make corn ethanol an issue.

As world food prices reach new highs, a handful of U.S. politicians and hard-hit corporations are readying a fresh effort to forestall the use of more U.S. corn and soybeans as motor fuel.

They are likely doing so in vain, say experts.

Unlike in 2008, when a wave of global panic over grain supplies provoked a fierce "food vs fuel" debate, there's so far only muted outcry over biofuels, even after corn surged last week [February 2011] to within 10 percent of its 2008 peak following a forecast showing even higher use in the ethanol sector.

The Challenge of Changing Ethanol Policy

While that may yet change as higher prices fuel inflation and trigger worried over supply security, officials and experts say ethanol is too ingrained in public policy and the economy of the U.S. heartland to be easily dislodged.

"What would it take for this public policy to be altered— The answer—a lot," said Gary Blumenthal of World Perspectives, a private consultant.

"The best voices for demanding change are U.S. consumers themselves, but that will require a food price spike larger than the 2 to 3 percent currently forecast by USDA [US Department of Agriculture]. And since the Fed [Federal Reserve] focuses on core inflation and ignores food and energy, it gets ignored there as well."

U.S. ethanol production this year [2011] will consume 15 percent of the world's corn supply, up from 10 percent in 2008. That share will continue to rise as the industry faces a mandate to boost minimum production an additional 20 percent by 2015. And exports are booming thanks to costly sugar-based rivals.

Attacking Corn Ethanol

Ethanol has become a lightning rod for criticism from opponents including foodmakers, livestock feeders, environmentalists and budget hawks.

The largest U.S. meatpacker, Tyson Foods Inc, which also raises chickens, and No. 1 pork processor Smithfield Foods Inc, which raises hogs, say ethanol drives up feed costs sharply and hurts consumers.

"It makes a lot more sense for us to burn our trash than burn our feed," Tyson CEO Donnie Smith said last month [January 2011].

As yet, foes have not found an electric argument to compel broad-scale change.

Food Security

On the global stage, the hand-wringing over soaring prices has focused on markets, not biofuel.

French President Nicolas Sarkozy, who has made food security a centerpiece of his one-year term leading the Group of 20 leading economies, has called for rules to curb commodity volatility, not to roll back widespread efforts to convert more crops to fuel.

Backtracking on existing ethanol mandates would be almost unthinkable at this point.

That finding has the support of a World Bank study released last July, that said: "The effect of biofuels on food prices has not been as large as originally thought, but that the use of commodities by financial investors . . . may have been partly responsible for the 2007–08 spike."

But with spending cuts the top issue for lawmakers this year, ethanol subsidies may be swept into the deficit debate.

"Before this (debate) is over . . . I suspect a lot of things will be looked at," said House Agriculture Committee Chairman Frank Lucas of Oklahoma, where major industries are ranching and oil and gas—two sectors skeptical of ethanol.

No Going Back

Backtracking on existing ethanol mandates would be almost unthinkable at this point. At same 900,000 barrels per day (bpd), ethanol now makes up about 10 percent of the gasoline pool in the world's largest oil consumer.

"The fact is the industry has pretty much been built," Joe Glauber said this week. "This isn't a question of just saying 'cut it off.' It's much more complicated than that."

And food prices, at least at home, have yet to pinch.

Prices at U.S. grocery stores and restaurants shot up 5.5 percent in 2008 without inspiring an ethanol overhaul. They were a negligible 1.8 percent in 2009 and a tiny 0.8 percent last year, so 2.5 percent may seem large this year. The overall inflation rate is forecast for 1.9 percent.

A Lack of Political Will

Nor is there great political will to make it an issue.

Republicans, including the Tea Party caucus, pushing for deep budget cuts, could single out the 45-cents-a-gallon fuel tax credit that encourages biofuel production, and helps ensure the sector remains profitable.

But at $6 billion a year, they are a drop in the U.S. budget bucket, and overturning them would likely face stiff opposition from President Barack Obama—whose determination to boost domestic resources is as resolute as his predecessors.

"Biofuels continue to be an important component of our clean energy strategy," a White House spokesman said when asked about ethanol, tight corn supplies and rising food prices.

"These home-grown, renewable fuels reduce our dependence on oil and create jobs and rural economic development."

Besides the tax credits, a 2007 law guarantees renewable fuels a rising share of the market. For corn ethanol, the mandate is 12.6 billion gallons this year and 15 billion gallons annually from 2015.

Production is set to reach 13.5 billion gallons this year—up 46 percent from 9.235 billion gallons in 2008. Makers will exceed the mandate this year due to exports and profit-making moments when ethanol is cheaper than gasoline.

Texas Unsuccessfully Sought Mandate Cut

When grain prices skyrocketed in 2008, Texas, home of the U.S. oil industry, asked the Bush administration to halve the ethanol mandate for that year. The request was rejected.

Last year [2010], Congress battled over ethanol subsidies before approving a one-year extension. Senator Dianne Feinstein of California is working on legislation to trim ethanol subsidies. "Federal subsidies and tariffs for ethanol are wrong for our fiscal policy and wrong for the environment and rising commodity prices are another indicator of that," she said.

"It's unfathomable that the corn ethanol industry can continue to assert that using 40 percent of the corn crop has no impact on food stocks or commodity prices," said the Environmental Working Group, an ethanol critic.

Ethanol defenders say that critique ignores the benefit of distillers dried grains, an ethanol co-product that can substitute for corn in livestock rations. Forty million tons of grains are available at lower cost than corn, they say.

The Politics of Corn Ethanol

Comparatively small numbers of lawmakers oppose corn ethanol, while farm-state lawmakers are a strong bloc of support. Last year [2010], the argument centered on possible cuts in the tax credits rather than elimination of them.

The major U.S. makers are privately owned POET, Archer Daniels Midland Co and Valero Energy Corp.

Advanced biofuels, such as ethanol from cellulose found in grass and woody plants, are the darling of corn ethanol critics. But the next-generation fuels amount to only a trickle of output and will need years to grow.

"Without ethanol, you have to have 10 percent more gas derived from oil. If you look at the impact on consumers, it would be huge," said Tom Buis of the ethanol trade group Growth Energy.

10

The US Corn Ethanol Subsidy Is Harmful

Robert Bryce

Robert Bryce is an author and a senior fellow at the Manhattan Institute.

The Deepwater Horizon oil spill in 2010 provided an opportunity for the US corn ethanol industry to capitalize on the disaster to push for more subsidies and mandates. The industry has been so heavily subsidized already that there is a glut of corn ethanol on the market. To get rid of the oversupply, the ethanol industry lobbied for a bailout, which came in a significant increase to the blend rate, the ratio of ethanol that can be mixed with conventional gasoline and then sold on the US market. More ethanol in the blend will cause damage to cars, boats, and other machines fueled by gasoline.

The most disgusting aspect of the blowout in the Gulf of Mexico [the Deepwater Horizon oil spill that dumped millions of barrels of oil into the Gulf of Mexico] isn't the video images of oil-soaked birds or the incessant blather from pundits about what BP [British Petroleum] or the Obama administration should be doing to stem the flow of oil. Instead, it's the ugly spectacle of the corn-ethanol scammers doing all they can to capitalize on the disaster so that they can justify an expansion of the longest-running robbery of taxpayers in U.S. history.

Listen to Matt Hartwig, communications director for the Renewable Fuels Association, an ethanol industry lobby group: "The Gulf of Mexico disaster serves as a stark and unfortunate reminder of the need for domestically-produced renewable biofuels." Or look at an advertisement that was . . . placed in a Washington, D.C., Metro station: "No beaches have been closed due to ETHANOL spills. . . . America's CLEAN fuel." That gem was paid for by Growth Energy, another ethanol industry lobby group.

The blowout of BP's Macondo well has given the corn-ethanol industry yet another opportunity to push its fuel adulterant on the American consumer. And unfortunately, the Obama administration appears ready and willing to foist yet more of the corrosive, environmentally destructive, low-heat-energy fuel on motorists.

The Corn Ethanol Scam

Why does the ethanol business need federal help? The answer is so disheartening that after five years of reporting on the corn-ethanol scam, I find it difficult to type, but here goes: The corn-ethanol industry needs to be bailed out by taxpayers because the industry was given too much in the way of subsidies and mandates. And now the only way to solve that problem is—what else?—more subsidies and mandates. The BP mess provides the industry with the opening it needs to win those subsidies from the federal government.

In its 2005 energy bill, Congress dramatically increased the mandates (and subsidies) for corn ethanol. That resulted in a surge of new construction. Led by German financial giant WestLB AG, banks poured billions of dollars into new distilleries, which quickly created an ethanol bubble that mirrored the U.S. real estate bubble. Over the past five years, U.S. ethanol production capacity has more than tripled and now stands at more than 13 billion gallons per year. But that's far more capacity than the U.S. motor fuel market can absorb. In March

[2010], nearly 1 billion gallons of ethanol production capacity was sitting idle. And yet, according to the Renewable Fuels Association, the industry has about 1.4 billion gallons of additional distilling capacity under construction.

The bankruptcy court is the best place to comprehend the oversupply of ethanol. Over the past 18 months or so, bankruptcy casualties have included VeraSun, the second-largest producer in the United States; Pacific Ethanol; Aventine Renewable Energy; and others.

The BP [British Petroleum] mess provides the industry with the opening it needs to win those subsidies from the federal government.

The "Blend Wall"

In industry parlance, the corn-ethanol sector is facing a head-on collision with the "blend wall." Ethanol producers depend on gasoline sales because their product must be mixed with conventional fuel. But thanks to the recession and the end of Americans' love affair with large SUVs, U.S. gasoline demand is flat or declining. That has left a smaller pool of gasoline to absorb all the alcohol the ethanol industry is producing. Or as Bob Dinneen, the president of the Renewable Fuels Association, has put it, "[W]e have lots of gallons of ethanol chasing too few gallons of gasoline."

Now the industry is counting on a president beleaguered by the made-for-TV crisis in the Gulf of Mexico to help it out. And he appears ready to do just that. On April 28, [2010] six days after the Deepwater Horizon rig sank, President Obama visited an ethanol plant in Missouri and declared that "there shouldn't be any doubt that renewable, homegrown fuels are a key part of our strategy for a clean-energy future." Obama also said, "I didn't just discover the merits of biofuels like ethanol when I first hopped on the campaign bus."

The strongest indication that an ethanol bailout is imminent came last Friday [June 4, 2010] when Agriculture Secretary Tom Vilsack (former governor of Iowa, the nation's biggest ethanol-producing state) said, "I'm very confident that we're going to see an increase in the blend rate."

The "blend rate" refers to the federal rule that limits ethanol blends to no more than 10 percent for standard automobiles. Commonly known as "E10," the fuel contains 90 percent gasoline and 10 percent alcohol. The Obama administration bailout, which would come via approval from the EPA [Environmental Protection Agency], will likely allow gasoline retailers to blend up to 15 percent ethanol into U.S. gasoline supplies.

[I]ncreased use of ethanol in gasoline will result in worse air quality.

The Damage of the Bailout

And that's where the corn-ethanol mess becomes truly outrageous and depressing. The United States now has about 250 million motor vehicles. Of that number, only about 7.5 million are designed to burn gasoline containing more than 10 percent ethanol. And there is evidence that even 10 percent ethanol may be too much for the other 242.5 million. Last year, Toyota recalled more than 200,000 Lexus vehicles because of internal component corrosion that was caused by ethanol-blended fuel.

In addition to problems with their cars, consumers may soon find that more ethanol in their gasoline will result in the fouling of smaller engines. The Outdoor Power Equipment Institute, which represents companies that make lawnmowers, snowblowers, chainsaws, and the like, opposes the bailout of the ethanol industry. It says that increasing the amount of ethanol in gasoline "could damage millions of forestry, lawn and garden, and other small engine products currently housed in consumers' garages."

The Critics

An increase in the ethanol blend rate is opposed by one of the oddest coalitions in modern American history. Last year [2009], more than 50 groups—including the Sierra Club, National Petrochemical and Refiners Association, Competitive Enterprise Institute, Grocery Manufacturers Association, Friends of the Earth, National Chicken Council, and the Association of International Automobile Manufacturers—signed a letter that was sent to Vilsack, EPA administrator Lisa Jackson, Energy Secretary Steven Chu, and Obama's energy advisor, Carol Browner. The coalition members said that they oppose "any administrative or legislative efforts to increase the current cap on the amount of ethanol permitted to be blended into gasoline" until "comprehensive testing programs" have been done.

Air Quality

The damage caused by increasing use of ethanol won't be limited to ruined boats, snowblowers, weed whackers, and lawnmowers. The EPA itself has admitted that increased use of ethanol in gasoline will result in worse air quality. You read that correctly: The agency in charge of protecting the environment in America concluded in April 2007 that total emissions of key air pollutants such as volatile organic compounds and nitrogen oxides will increase because of expanded use of ethanol.

Food Supplies

Yes, it's madness. And none of this even considers the effect that the ethanol rip-off is having on food supplies. Earlier this year, the Earth Policy Institute estimated that in 2009, the U.S.

ethanol industry consumed 107 million tons of grain, or about 25 percent of total domestic grain production. That amount of grain, said the Institute, "was enough to feed 330 million people for one year at average world consumption levels."

BP's disaster in the Gulf of Mexico will force the offshore oil and gas industry to dramatically improve its safety procedures. That's a good thing. But if it only serves to strengthen the corn-ethanol industry, it will be a squandered opportunity, and another tragedy for the nation.

11

The Cellulosic Ethanol Industry Needs More Government Support

Tom Doggett

Tom Doggett is an energy correspondent for Reuters.

Although President George W. Bush pledged that the cellulosic ethanol industry would be competitive by 2012, it has failed to meet expectations. The industry's slow growth is due to the US government's reluctance to assure much-needed investors that there will be long-term government subsidies for research and development. Another reason for the stagnation is that Congress has not set big enough mandates to encourage more production of cellulosic ethanol. Congress needs to provide incentives for venture capital investors to bet on production plants.

The great promise of a car fuel made from cheap, clean-burning prairie grass or wood chips—and not from expensive corn that feeds the world—is more mirage than reality.

Despite years of research, testing and some hype, the next-generation ethanol industry is far from the commercial success envisioned by President George W. Bush in 2006, when he pledged so-called cellulosic biofuels would be "practical and competitive" by 2012. Instead the only real alternative to traditional gasoline is ethanol made from corn, a fuel environmentalists say is not green at all because of the energy-intensive nature of modern farming.

A Failure of Policy

Critics say it is a failure of government policy, not science, that the U.S. is still so dependent on corn for its biofuels. Washington has backtracked on cellulosic ethanol production targets and failed to provide assurances to investors that the sector would be subsidized over the long term.

While there are dozens of pilot and demonstration cellulosic ethanol projects around the country, the groundwork for the first commercial plants is only now getting underway. Battered by recession, funding remains scarce for $100-million-plus plants needed for commercial-scale production so cellulosic can compete against cheaper ethanol-based corn.

"The earliest you're going to see efficient cellulosic ethanol is five years," said Richard Brock, president of Brock Associates, an advisory firm in Milwaukee.

Washington has backtracked on cellulosic ethanol production targets and failed to provide assurances to investors that the sector would be subsidized over the long term.

Assurances Required

For the industry to take off, investors need to be reassured that Congress will extend a cellulosic production tax credit for several years and cellulosic output targets will be big enough to encourage blenders to lock in future capacity.

"It would certainly increase volumes at a faster rate than what we've seen in the last couple of years," said Mac Statton, biofuels analyst with the Energy Department's forecasting arm.

Gasoline in the United States is blended with up to 15 percent ethanol, which helps reduce oil imports.

In the short term, however, the cellulosic industry's slow growth will make little difference to either America's addiction to foreign crude oil or the strains on corn supplies that critics claim have pushed up food prices.

A Failed Mandate

Cellulosic biofuels production was supposed to reach 500 million gallons next year under federal mandates that rise each year until it eventually passes corn-based ethanol output. But no cellulosic production is expected this year and it may grow to only a few million gallons next year.

Because the cellulosic industry is not able to meet the production goals mandated by Congress, the Environmental Protection Agency [EPA] has the authority to lower them. That's what the agency did this month [July 2011] for the third straight year when it proposed lowering the original half billion gallon target for 2012 to between 3.6 million and 15.7 million gallons. EPA issues the final target in November [2010].

The Energy Department doesn't expect cellulosic output to reach its first 1 billion gallons until 2018. Congress, under its mandates, wants 7 billion gallons that year.

The industry has made great progress in bringing down the production costs of cellulosic ethanol from $5 to $6 a gallon a decade ago to as low as $2.50. However, the first cellulosic plants are expensive to build and will add to that $2.50 cost, putting cellulosic slightly above corn ethanol's cost.

Government Help for Commercial-Scale Plants

Coskata Inc. was given a $250 million federal loan guarantee in January [2010] to build a 55-million-gallon a year plant in Alabama to process wood biomass into ethanol. POET LLC, the world's biggest ethanol producer, was awarded a $105 million loan guarantee this month for a plant in Iowa to produce 25 million gallons of ethanol from corn cobs starting in 2013.

Other companies aiming to produce big volumes of cellulosic ethanol or provide enzymes that break down cellulose feedstocks are DuPont's Genencor, Abengoa Bioenergy, Qteros and Novozymes A/S.

About $1.5 billion in venture capital poured into the cellulosic industry to help fund initial pilot projects over the last decade, according to the Advanced Ethanol Coalition that lobbies for the industry.

A Big Question Mark

As cellulosic producers move to large-scale operations, venture capital investors are reluctant to bet on the expensive $150 million plants, said Brooke Coleman, who heads the coalition.

"The venture capital guys will spend $20 million or $30 million on you in the start-up phase," he said. "They don't build plants and like to get in and get out in five years."

It is the big banks, oil firms and major energy companies that will help finance the new commercial-scale plants, but many are scared off by the uncertainty over the $1.01 tax credit and changes in production goals.

Analysts argue that with oil prices high, it should be easier for cellulosic biofuels to attract investors, but incentives from Congress are a big question mark.

A draft bill unveiled in the Senate would extend the $1.01 per gallon tax credit for three years and add ethanol made from algae to the list of cellulosic biofuels eligible to get it.

Where's the Incentive?

Extending the credit for cellulosic ethanol is part of a compromise for Congress to end a 45-cent-a-gallon tax credit for corn ethanol, which is exceeding its production targets.

But with lawmakers looking to cut government spending, cellulosic producers may be lucky to get a one-year extension.

"How the hell do you extend a tax credit for a multi-year period, when there's no money in the Treasury," said Christine Tezak, energy analyst at Robert W. Baird.

All the uncertainties, however, hurt the industry. Refineries that blend the fuel don't have a reason to sign long-term contracts with biofuels producers, which would encourage investment in new plants and boost output.

"There's no incentive for anybody on the consuming side to ring up a cellulosic guy and say: 'Hey, I'd like to take care of my renewable fuel standard obligations for the next five years, so I need to secure not only present but future production capacity with you,'" said Tezak.

12

The US Must Reconsider Subsidizing Inefficient and Harmful Biofuels

C. Ford Runge

C. Ford Runge is a professor at the University of Minnesota and a fellow at the Hubert H. Humphrey Institute of Public Affairs.

Despite mounting evidence that biofuels are harmful to the environment, exacerbate climate change, and threaten the world's food supply, the US government continues to subsidize the industry and set mandates for biofuel production. This is a testament to the powerful farm lobby in the Unites States. Congress must reassess its policies and implement a freeze on further mandates, cut tariff protection and subsidies, and put in place government initiatives to develop more sustainable forms of renewable energy.

In light of the strong evidence that growing corn, soybeans, and other food crops to produce ethanol takes a heavy toll on the environment and is hurting the world's poor through higher food prices, consider this astonishing fact: This year [2010], more than a third of the U.S.'s record corn harvest of 335 million metric tons will be used to produce corn ethanol. What's more, within five years fully 50 percent of the U.S. corn crop is expected to wind up as biofuels.

Here's another sobering fact. Despite the record deficits facing the U.S., and notwithstanding President Obama's embrace of some truly sustainable renewable energy policies, the president and his administration have wholeheartedly embraced corn ethanol and the tangle of government subsidies, price supports, and tariffs that underpin the entire dubious enterprise of using corn to power our cars. In early February [2010], the president threw his weight behind new and existing initiatives to boost ethanol production from both food and nonfood sources, including supporting Congressional mandates that would triple biofuel production to 36 billion gallons by 2022.

Congress and the Obama administration are paying billions of dollars to producers of biofuels, with expenditures scheduled to increase steadily through 2022 and possibly 2030. The fuels are touted by these producers as a "green" solution to reliance on imported petroleum, and a boost for farmers seeking higher prices.

Facing the Truth

Yet a close look at their impact on food security and the environment—with profound effects on water, the eutrophication of our coastal zones from fertilizers, land use, and greenhouse gas emissions—suggests that the biofuel bandwagon is anything but green. Congress and the administration need to reconsider whether they are throwing good money after bad. If the biofuel saga illustrates anything, it is that thinking ecologically will require thinking more logically, as well.

Investments in biofuels have grown rapidly in the last decade, accelerating especially in developed countries and Brazil after 2003, when oil prices began to climb above $25 per barrel, reaching a peak of $120 per barrel in 2008. Between 2001 and 2008, world production of ethanol tripled from 4.9 billion gallons to 17 billion gallons, while biodiesel output rose from 264 million gallons to 2.9 billion gallons. Together, the U.S. and Brazil account for most of the world's ethanol production. Biodiesel, the other major biofuel, is produced mainly in the European Union [EU], which makes roughly five times more than the U.S. In the EU, ethanol and biodiesel are projected to increase oilseed, wheat, and corn usage from negligible levels in 2004 to roughly 21, 17, and 5 million tons, respectively, in 2016, according to the Organization for Economic Cooperation and Development.

The Role of Government Subsidies

In the U.S., once a reliable supplier of exported grain and oilseeds for food, biofuel production is soaring even as food crop export demand remains strong, driving prices further upward. Government support undergirding the biofuels industry has also grown rapidly and now forms a massive federal program that may be good for farm states, but is very bad for U.S. taxpayers.

If the biofuel saga illustrates anything, it is that thinking ecologically will require thinking more logically, as well.

These subsidy supports are a testament to the power of the farm lobby and its sway over the U.S. Congress. In addition to longstanding crop price supports that encourage production of corn and soybeans as feedstocks, biofuels are propped up by several other forms of government largesse. The first of these are mandates, known as "renewable fuels standards": In the U.S. in 2007, energy legislation raised mandated production of biofuels to 36 billion gallons by 2022. These mandates shelter biofuels investments by guaranteeing that the demand will be there, thus encouraging oversupply.

Then there are direct biofuel production subsidies, which raise feedstock prices for farmers by increasing the price of corn. In the U.S., blenders are paid a 45 cent-per-gallon "blender's tax credit" for ethanol—the equivalent of more than $200 per acre to divert scarce corn from the food supply into fuel tanks. The federal government also pays a $1 credit for plant-based biodiesel and "cellulosic" ethanol.

Finally, there is a 54 cent-per-gallon tariff on imported biofuel to protect domestic production from competition, especially to prevent Brazilian sugarcane-based ethanol (which can be produced at less than half the cost of U.S. ethanol from corn) from entering U.S. markets. These subsidies allow ethanol producers to pay higher and higher prices for feedstocks, illustrated by the record 2008 levels of corn, soybean, and wheat prices. Projections suggest they will remain higher, assuming normal weather and yields.

The Impact of Food Supply on Food Prices

The rapid increase in grain and oilseed prices due to biofuels expansion has been a shock to consumers worldwide, especially during 2008 and early 2009. From 2005 to January 2008, the global price of wheat increased 143 percent, corn by 105 percent, rice by 154 percent, sugar by 118 percent, and oilseeds by 197 percent. In 2006–2007, this rate of increase accelerated, according to the U.S. Department of Agriculture, "due to continued demand for biofuels and drought in major producing countries." The price increases have since moderated, but many believe only temporarily, given tight stocks-to-use ratios.

It is in poor countries that these price increases pose direct threats to disposable income and food security. There, the run-up in food prices has been ominous for the more than one billion of the world's poor who are chronically food-insecure. Poor farmers in countries such as Bangladesh can barely support a household on a subsistence basis, and have little if any surplus production to sell, which means they do not benefit from higher prices for corn or wheat. And poor slum-dwellers in Lagos, Calcutta, Manila, or Mexico City produce no food at all, and spend as much as 90 percent of their meager household incomes just to eat.

The Environmental Impact

But the most worrisome of recent criticisms of biofuels relate to their impacts on the natural environment. In the U.S., water shortages due to the huge volumes necessary to process grains or sugar into ethanol are not uncommon, and are amplified if these crops are irrigated. Growing corn to produce ethanol, according to a 2007 study by the U.S. National Academy of Sciences, consumes 200 times more water than the water used to process corn into ethanol.

In the cornbelt of the Upper Midwest, even more serious problem arise. Corn acreage, which expanded by over 15 percent in 2007 in response to ethanol demands, requires extensive fertilization, adding to nitrogen and phosphorus that run off into lakes and streams and eventually enter the Mississippi River watershed. This is aggravated by systems of subterranean tiles and drains—98 percent of Iowa's arable fields are tiled—that accelerate field drainage into ditches and local watersheds. As a result, loadings of nitrogen and phosphorus into the Mississippi and the Gulf of Mexico encourage algae growth, starving water bodies of oxygen needed by aquatic life and enlarging the hypoxic "dead zone" in the gulf.

Thus have biofuels made the slow fade from green to brown.

Next is simply the crop acreage needed to feed the biofuels beast. A 2007 study in *Science* noted that to replace just 10 percent of the gasoline in the U.S. with ethanol and biodiesel would require 43 percent of current U.S. cropland for biofuel feedstocks. The EU [European Union] would need to commit 38 percent of its cropland base. Otherwise, new lands will need to be brought into cultivation, drawn disproportionately from those more vulnerable to environmental damage, such as forests.

A pair of 2008 studies, again in *Science*, focused on the question of greenhouse gas emissions due to land-use shifts resulting from biofuels. One study said that if land is converted from rainforests, peatlands, savannas, or grasslands to produce biofuels, it causes a large net increase in greenhouse gas emissions for decades. A second study said that growing corn for ethanol in the U.S., for example, can lead to the clearing of forests and other wild lands in the developing world for food corn, which also causes a surge in greenhouse gas emissions.

A third study, by Nobel-Prize winning chemist Paul Crutzen in 2007, emphasized the impact from the heavy applications of nitrogen needed to grow expanded feedstocks of corn and rapeseed. The nitrogen necessary to grow these crops releases nitrous oxide into the atmosphere—a greenhouse gas 296 times more damaging than CO_2—and contributes more to global warming than biofuels save through fossil fuel reductions.

A Reassessment of Government Policy Is Vital

Thus have biofuels made the slow fade from green to brown. It is a sad irony of the biofuels experience that resource alternatives that seemed farmer-friendly and green have turned out so badly.

What's needed are a freeze on further mandates to slow overinvestment, reductions in the blenders' tax credit—especially when corn prices are high—and cuts in tariff protection to encourage cost-reduction strategies by U.S. producers. And the high environmental and human costs of using corn, soybeans, and other food crops to produce biofuels should spur government initiatives to develop more sustainable forms of renewable energy, such as wind power, solar power, and—one day, perhaps—algal biofuels grown at waste treatment plants.

Yet sadly, as in so many areas of policy, Congress and the administration prefer to reward inefficiency and political influence more than pursuing cost-effective—and sustainable—energy strategies.

13

Algae Is a Good Source for Biodiesel

Elizabeth Svoboda

Elizabeth Svoboda is a contributing editor at Popular Science.

Algae holds a lot of potential as the next great fuel source. It has several advantages over other crops: It can be grown in an enclosed space, it grows effectively and quickly, and it is better for the environment. Although there are many challenges to developing the technology, the payoff may be huge for investors and consumers.

"Here it is!" Jim Sears says with a tour guide's come-see enthusiasm. I stop, my feet stuck in six inches of fresh powder outside the Old Fort Collins power plant, but the contraption before us doesn't exactly inspire awe. Two parallel tracks, each about 60 feet long, protrude from the snow like the twin runners of a giant upended sled. A washing-machine-size box studded with dials and blank displays sits at one end. Nothing moves, nothing glows, nothing hums. The future of alternative energy sits silent before me. This is what's going to make gasoline obsolete?

Sears chuckles at my confusion. "Nothing's really set up at the moment," he explains. "The bags aren't hooked up. We don't want to damage the equipment by letting it sit in the snow." My eyes drift to the only spot of color in the entire crystalline scene: a wide acrylic tank off to the side that looks like an aquarium left to ferment in the windowsill. The water inside is seaweed green and so opaque it's almost milky. I run my finger over the top, brushing off snow as I go. "What's in here?" I ask. Sears eyes the tank fondly. "This is the first step," he says. "This is where the algae starts to grow."

Little Giants

Algae seems a strange contender for the mantle of World's Next Great Fuel, but the green goop has several qualities in its favor. Algae, made up of simple aquatic organisms that capture light energy through photosynthesis, produces vegetable oil. Vegetable oil, in turn, can be transformed into biodiesel, which can be used to power just about any diesel engine. (There are currently 13 million of them on American roads, a number that's expected to jump over the next decade.)

Algae has some important advantages over other oil-producing crops, like canola and soybeans. It can be grown in almost any enclosed space, it multiplies like gangbusters, and it requires very few inputs to flourish—mainly just sunlight, water and carbon dioxide. "Because algae has a high surface-area-to-volume ratio, it can absorb nutrients very quickly," Sears says. "Its small size is what makes it mighty."

Algae seems a strange contender for the mantle of World's Next Great Fuel, but the green goop has several qualities in its favor.

The proof is in the numbers. About 140 billion gallons of biodiesel would be needed every year to replace all petroleum-based transportation fuel in the U.S. It would take nearly three billion acres of fertile land to produce that amount with soybeans, and more than one billion acres to produce it with canola. Unfortunately, there are only 434 million acres of cropland in the entire country, and we probably want to reserve some of that to grow food. But because of its ability to propagate almost virally in a small space, algae could do the job in just 95 million acres of land. What's more, it doesn't need fertile soil to thrive. It grows in ponds, bags or tanks that can be just as easily set up in the desert—or next to a carbon-dioxide-spewing power plant—as in the country's breadbasket.

Sears claims that these efficiencies will allow Solix Biofuels, the company he founded, to create algae-based biodiesel that costs about the same as gasoline. But like any start-up trying to carve a niche in the post-oil age, Solix must struggle for answers before it can sell a thing: Which species of algae will produce the most oil? What's the best way to it? And not least, how do you extract the oil from the algae once it's grown? The research and debate at solix is so fierce that it has already claimed one casualty—my guide, Jim Sears.

A Fresh Start

Sears, an engineer-turned-inventor, started developing his algae-fuel technology in 2004, but the events that inspired his venture stretch back to the last time the U.S. faced an energy crisis. In 1978 President Carter established the Aquatic Species Program (ASP), a research initiative charged with developing biodiesel from algae as a clean, homegrown alternative to gasoline. Yet some two decades and $25 million later, the team had failed to produce any significant amount of oil from algae, and in 1996 the Clinton administration axed the program. Still, the researchers hoped their work would not go to waste. "The directors were adamant that we make available a detailed summary of what we'd done, because they knew that in the future someone would be interested," says John Sheehan, a former ASP project scientist. Sheehan and his colleagues compiled a 328-page report on their work and uploaded it to a Department of Energy Web site.

At the time, Sears was working on a smorgasbord of projects in his garage, including a cattle "hump-o-meter" (his term) intended to tell farmers when their animals were mating. He had spent time as an engineer with the Navy in the 1980s, designing, among other things, sonar equipment that helped SEAL divers find pieces of the space shuttle Challenger wreck. During this stint he made an unforgettable nighttime dive off the coast of Florida. As he treaded water, streams of phosphorescent algae drifted past him, tracing trails of light in the murk as far as he could see.

Two decades later, Sears, looking for a new project, found himself reliving that one sublime dive. He wondered if algae like that could create enough energy to help solve the fuel crisis. A little online research turned up the ASP report.

It was a revelation. Sears pored over the "Algae Bible," as he now calls it, for weeks, determined to find the reason for the gap between the program's potential and its results. "I started thinking, 'Well, if this is as great as it sounds, why aren't we all driving around with algae fuel in our tanks?'" He noticed that ASP researchers had tried to grow the unique oil-producing algae in open ponds, which were far cheaper to maintain than closed systems like a sealed aquarium. But wild algae quickly invaded these open ponds and took over, outcompeting their obese counterparts.

A New Approach

Sears's solution was inspired by the most humble of kitchen implements, the Ziploc bag. Clear plastic sacks, he realized, would let in enough light to help the algae thrive yet prevent unwanted species from invading. The crux of his innovation is his design for a full-scale algae "reactor." Two 350-foot-long parallel tracks about three feet apart hold the bags in place. Custom-built rollers occasionally squeeze them like tubes of toothpaste, circulating the algae; a current gives them the intermittent sun exposure they need to flourish. Once the algae is grown, a refinery extracts its oil and converts it to biodiesel. Sears tried to sell his idea to venture capitalists and found them skeptical at best. In an effort to shore up his credibility, Sears approached Bryan Willson, the director of Colorado State University's Engines and Energy Conversion Laboratory. The first time Sears visited the lab—housed in the converted Old Fort Collins power plant—he knew he had found a kindred spirit. When they sat down together to go over the Algae Bible, Sears recalls, they each produced their own well-worn copy. "I had tons of yellow stickies on mine, and he had tons of yellow stickies on his." Sears convinced Willson (along with his gaggle of graduate students) to sign on to the project and join his fledgling company.

Money, Power, Politics

Nowadays, no one questions the need to quickly develop viable alternatives to petroleum. The U.S. vehicle fleet pumps 1.3 billlion tons of carbon dioxide into the atmosphere every year, and we pay foreign governments and corporations $820 million a day for the oil needed to do so. As gas prices rise and the public becomes increasingly attuned to the unpleasant realities of global warming, even once-reluctant politicians are beginning to take action. In January's State of the Union address [2007], President Bush announced his "Twenty in Ten" plan to reduce American gasoline usage by 20 percent in the next 10 years. The plan sets mandatory standards to raise production of renewable fuels to 35 billion gallons per year by 2017.

With the political tides changing, investors smell money in the water. No one knows for sure if the alternative-fuel economy will be led by ethanol, plug-in hybrids, biofuel or none of the above, so venture capitalists are betting on everything. It's a good time to be in algae. Heavy hitters like biotech's big backer Craig Venter, Bob Metcalfe of Polaris Venture Partners and Steve Jurvetson of Draper Fisher Jurvetson have distributed millions of dollars of seed money to an assortment of green-ooze-growing firms, including GreenFuel,

Aurora Biofuels and Solazyme. Doug Henston, the former investment banker and real-estate manager who Sears brought on board as chief operating officer of Solix in 2006, recently secured $2 million in funding from Bohemian Investments.

Algae Investment

One advantage algae start-ups have over other alternative-fuel companies is that, by feeding carbon dioxide from power plants to the algae, they could help utility companies manage their emissions as well. The European Union already regulates carbon dioxide emissions, and there are currently four bills being considered in the U.S. Senate that would impose similar restrictions. Another start-up, GreenFuel, which originated at the Massachusetts Institute of Technology, has used CO_2 from a power plant to grow its algae. "Our experiment was a success," says Ray Hobbs, a senior consulting engineer at Arizona Public Service, one of GreenFuel's utility partners. "We've only produced a very small amount of fuel so far-we were just out to verify the concept-but we now know that this is doable."

Nowadays, no one questions the need to quickly develop viable alternatives to petroleum.

Ultimately, though, the success of algae biodiesel, like every other alternative fuel, will rely on whether the market price of fossil fuels reflects their environmental costs. "The real unknown is, what is the future of carbon going to be?" Sheehan says. "Will it have a cost in the marketplace?" Martin Tobias, a venture capitalist at the Ignition Partners firm, is more direct about how important carbon regulation is. "The success of this industry will depend on the price of oil," he says. "If oil drops back down to $20 a barrel, you're going to see all the wind come out of these companies' sails."

Pick a Species, Any Species

If you tossed a Ben & Jerry's scoop shop and a Munich beer hall in a blender, you'd get a pretty close approximation of the New Belgium Brewery in Fort Collins. There are more cruiser bikes in the parking lot than cars, and bright colors and tie-dye are de rigueur attire for staffers and patrons alike. Our server greets us above the din and offers us tasting forms that we can use to request free samples-provided we also fill out a "personal expression" section featuring questions like "If you could be in any band, which one would you join, and what instrument would you play?" (Sears's answers: the Beatles, lead guitar.)

New Belgium is one of Sears's favorite places to unwind after an 80-hour workweek, so it's fitting that he decided to bring the brewery on board as a key part of Solix's future plans. As with a coal-fired utility, carbon dioxide is a copious by-product of the brewing process. Except, unlike a utility's, New Belgium's CO_2 is nearly pure, perfect for injecting into the test reactor that Solix plans to build on an empty stretch of New Belgium land. If all goes as planned, within the next year New Belgium will begin to feed gas directly into the plastic baggies, nourishing the fatty algae as it multiplies. It's a testbed, a proof of concept for the partnerships that Solix is negotiating with power plants.

> [T]he success of algae biodiesel . . . will rely on whether the market price of fossil fuels reflects their environmental costs.

The Right Stuff

Key to the project is picking the right type of algae. There are thousands of types of algae that could potentially produce the right kind of vegetable oil, and there are times when Amy

Boczon, a CSU [Colorado State University] graduate student in biology, feels like she has tried them all. Back at Solix's lab at the Old Fort Collins power plant, she swings open a refrigerator door to reveal test tubes crammed in like six-packs. Sears, Henston, Willson and I look them over. Each tube in the array is a slightly different shade of green, containing a distinct species of algae that Solix is evaluating for its fat-production potential.

Boczon's job is to manipulate the algae's environment to maximize the amount of oil it produces. "You need to make [it] think, 'Gosh, am I going to go through a time when I'm not going to have a certain nutrient?'" she explains. Yet switching the algae into oil-production mode by removing nutrients like nitrogen can also slow its growth and endanger its health. The trick is to harvest the cells at their peak—after they've accumulated maximum oil stores but before they succumb to overstress.

I cut to the chase. "So, how much fuel have you produced so far?"

Everyone looks askance at one another, as if I've violated some unspoken rule of conduct. Mark Machacek, another Solix employee, leaves the room for a moment and comes back with an Erlenmeyer flask. When he holds it up to the light, I can just make out a trace of brownish liquid, like the last drops of whiskey at the bottom of a tumbler. "That's it," he says. "That's all we've got."

It's Not Easy Being Green

The oil-smudged beaker is a vivid reminder of the challenges start-ups like Solix face. "Algae fuel is truly in the R&D stage, and to present it any other way at this point would be a mistake," says Jeff Probst, the CEO of BlueSun Biodiesel in Westminster, Colorado. BlueSun has expressed interest in using algae as a feedstock, but only if Solix can produce it in large enough quantities.

In theory, making fuel from algae should be straightforward. The government scientists who ran the Aquatic Species Program proved that it is possible to grow a whole bunch of green stuff and add chemicals to extract the oil and make at least a small amount of fuel. "This isn't cold fusion—it's not like nobody's done this before," Willson points out. But replicating and improving on 20-year-old results isn't all that easy. Out of the dozens of brash young algae-biodiesel start-ups, only one, Aquaflow in New Zealand, has managed to produce enough fuel to power a car engine.

This delay reflects the unique difficulties of engineering a biological system. Each algae-growing reactor is a miniature biosphere unto itself, built on the same delicate web of dependencies as a natural ecosystem. Change one element, and you can nudge others into disarray. "Algae is a holy grail because it can grow so quickly," says Cary Bullock, the CEO of Green-Fuel. "But for it to reach its potential, you have to make sure all the algae gets just the right amount of light. If there's too much or too little, you won't get a good enough yield." Spurring the algae on to Herculean growth rates, he adds, creates its own set of problems. The swiftly multiplying cells decimate the carbon dioxide supply they use to make food, and in large numbers, they block out the very light they need to survive.

Technology and Investment

These issues, Sears says, can be addressed with computer systems that limit growth rates by precisely controlling the amount of nutrients that are added to the tank. But making such refinements adds to capital costs, which threatens the bare-bones economic philosophy that algae fuel companies must embrace to make a product competitive with petroleum-based diesel.

After the harvest, another conundrum presents itself: how to get the oil out. Algae isn't fibrous enough to stand up to cold pressing, the standard way of extracting fat from plant matter. Processing the green slurry piped out of the bags by adding chemicals like methanol or hexane is the most obvious alternative-an efficient and relatively cheap means of removing oil. But some observers worry about the possible unintended consequences of the operation. "There are different schemes that are likely to affect land and water use and, if anything gets loose, there's a whole variety of possible impacts," says Dan Kammen, the director of the University of California at Berkeley's Renewable and Appropriate Energy Laboratory.

Each algae-growing reactor is a miniature biosphere unto itself, built on the same delicate web of dependencies as a natural ecosystem.

Sears also can't account for the other variables that will help determine Solix's fate. Will lawmakers see fit to subsidize algae fuel at the expense of other established alternatives, like ethanol? Will U.S. automakers ever manufacture cars that can run on biodiesel? "The tests that have been done so far show there's some promise," Probst says, "but it's not at the stage yet where you want to get people's expectations built up." It's a long way from a few drops at the bottom of a flask to powering America.

Hidden Casualties

Sears has learned firsthand how these challenges can affect more than the bottom line. Last November [2006], Willson, Henston and a representative of investor Bohemian Investments, not wanting to be bound to the specifics of Sears's original reactor design, voted Sears out as CEO. Henston assumed CEO status and control over the company's future research plans, and Sears lost his sure grasp on building the baggie-and-roller reactor he had originally conceived.

"Jim is a visionary," Willson says, "but I don't have any emotional attachment to his plans." The clear implication is that Sears might have blocked any changes to his original design, even if they were shown to improve the growing process. (Indeed, although Sears plans to maintain a working relationship with Solix, he is in the process of forming a separate company to pursue his original, unadulterated dream.) Later this year [2007], Solix will test a new prototype design that will not include rollers—which pose the risk of wearing out the plastic bags—to agitate the algae; instead, bubbles percolating through the green slurry will ensure that the mixture is sufficiently stirred. Additionally, new multitiered, triangle-shaped compartments inside the bags will reflect the sun's rays, illuminate the algae from multiple directions, and, ideally, bump up fuel yields.

It's been a long year for Sears, but he knows that Solix's future—like the future of algae biodiesel as a whole—depends on so much more than any one person can foresee. "Who knows," he says with characteristic equanimity, his ever-present smile playing around his lips. "Me being thrown out as CEO may turn out to be a great thing for the company."

14

Algae Is Not a Sustainable Source for Biodiesel

Gerd Klöck

Gerd Klöck is professor at Hochschule Bremen University in Germany.

Algae has been hailed as the next great fuel source. However, there are a number of major problems with the conversion process, the main one being that it takes too much energy to produce usable fuel. The fact that the practice is not sustainable at this time means that more research is needed to develop the technology to more efficiently grow, harvest, convert, and transport fuel created from algae.

Microalgae appear to be the answer to the world's energy problems as they hold out the promise of cheap, clean transport fuels without many of the problems that dog other biofuels. Algae can, at least in principle, produce large quantities of lipids using water resources, such as salt, waste and brackish water, which cannot usually be exploited, in areas that are unsuitable for conventional agriculture. This has sparked a new gold rush as companies seek to produce clean liquid fuels for an energy hungry world. But it may not be as simple to roll out this technology as it first appears.

In theory, producing biodiesel from algae should be a simple technical process. The algae can be harvested from the culture medium and dried so the lipids contained within can

Gerd Klöck, "It's the Process, Stupid," *Chemistry & Industry*, February 22, 2010. www .soci.org. Copyright © 2010 by John Wiley & Sons Ltd. All rights reserved. Reproduced by permission of John Wiley & Sons Ltd.

be extracted and, ultimately, converted into biodiesel. Various scientific groups and companies have demonstrated the feasibility of this procedure at laboratory scale and, in January 2009, a Continental Airways passenger aircraft even flew successfully for over an hour using a fuel mixture of algae and Jatropha oil.

The Process

Currently, microalgae can be cultured in so-called 'open ponds' and sealed photobioreactors. Open ponds consist of flat basins with about 20cm of water, in which a paddle mixes algae cultures in a circular motion, while photobioreactors are always sealed. For economic reasons, commercially produced microalgae are predominantly cultured in open ponds and the largest cultivation operations occupy several hectares.

[I]t may not be as simple to roll out this technology as it first appears.

Sunlight is the energy source behind microalgae growth and is the limiting factor for production. In Europe, the maximum theoretically attainable yield is approximately 100g microalgae/m² day, but around double this can be produced in the Sahara. Considering an average oil content of 33%, theoretically a maximum of about 10L of extractable algal oil could be produced per square metre. In the 1990s, researchers at the US National Renewable Energy Laboratory achieved an average of 15–20g of oil/m²/day during productive months. Average productivity over a period of several months resulted in yields that were about 20% of the thermodynamic maximum.

The Issue of Energy Balance

The question of energy balance is essential when calculating the sustainability of biomass production. How much energy is in the biomass and how much energy is required for production and refining? A kilogram of dried algae biomass has approximately 27MJ of energy in it. Using state of the art technology for mixing, pumping, cooling, harvesting, extracting and drying, at least 35–45MJ of energy must be expended in order to produce 27MJ energy.

This estimate does not take into account the many steps in the total production process of actual biofuels, such as biodiesel, which also requires energy. The energy costs for transport, supplying CO_2 to the cultures, preparation and regeneration of culture media and cleaning procedures, also needs to be taken into account. It also needs to be considered that each step in the process is accompanied by a certain loss factor. The above estimate operates with the unrealistic assumption of zero loss during the procedures.

The basic data used for this calculation are derived from practical experience at considerably smaller facilities. Higher energy costs are inevitable in larger facilities, possessing multiple square kilometres, as liquids, such as culture medium, will have to be transported over longer distances.

Other Problematic Issues

The negative energy balance is not the only problem when evaluating the sustainability of algae biodiesel. There are a range of other, unsolved problematic issues.

A new fuel source can only become commercially successful relatively quickly if it is compatible with existing infrastructure for the supply of fuel. The mineral oil industry's so-called 'economic target' for algae biodiesel is a price of $0.48/L and a 'minimum order' of 210m L. This corresponds to the annual consumption of about 200,000 vehicles. To fuel this many vehicles an algae culturing facility, using 20cm deep open ponds, would occupy at least 85 km². Since fast-growing algae are required for commercial production, a biomass doubling time of one day can be assumed. Accordingly, about half of the facility will need to be harvested daily, meaning that 8.6

m^3 of culture medium will need to be moved. It should be remarked that rapid growth and lipid content are negatively correlated with regard to microalgae. Fast-growing algae do not accumulate lipids; conditions of privation or stress are required to produce significant quantities of lipids.

Undesirable organisms, such as 'wild' algae, bacteria, protozoa and insects, are another problem in open ponds and could necessitate the use of herbicides or pesticides over large areas. It should be noted that highly toxic algae, which would suppress the growth of other types of algae could grow in culture, and even normally harmless algae may excrete toxic compounds under certain circumstances. As at least 3–10mm of liquid evaporate each day from open ponds, considerable quantities of fresh water will also be required to prevent salt concentrations from rising.

The land required for large facilities may not be suitable for agriculture; however, it may still be valuable to local populations. Infrequently used areas are also often valuable habitats for rare and protected plants and animals.

Not Sustainable at This Time

At first glance, microalgae appear to be an attractive source of biomass, but a more detailed consideration of energy requirements, however, indicates that the practice is not currently sustainable due to the negative energy balance associated with production. Culture stability, media recycling and harvesting are still significant hurdles to overcome and require further research. Field demonstration projects will also be needed to increase understanding of the possible environmental risks of large scale microalgal monocultures.

15

The European Union Is Reassessing Its Use of Biofuels

Charles Hawley

Charles Hawley is a correspondent for German news magazine Der Spiegel.

The European Union is taking into account the increasingly harsh criticisms against biofuels and has put some tough regulations in place, such as making it illegal to use biofuels from recently clear-cut forests. Scientists and environmentalists doubt that the costs associated with biofuels will ever be worth the gain. Many assert that biofuels are more harmful than conventional fossil fuels and call for a total moratorium on the use of biofuels.

The images are enough to soothe one's soul. Golden fields of grain stretching as far as the eye can see; bright yellow rapeseed flower blooming in the European countryside; drivers happily cruising down the autobahn, smiling in the knowledge that the biodiesel their car is burning does no harm to the environment.

But such a bucolic view of biofuels—gas and diesel made from plants—may soon become a thing of the past. The European Union [EU] on Wednesday [January 16, 2008] unveiled a far-reaching plan aimed at cutting greenhouse gas emissions by 20 percent relative to 1990 and dramatically upping the share of renewable energies in the 27-member bloc's energy mix. The scheme also calls for 10 percent of fuel used in transportation to be made up of biofuels. That last element, though, is becoming increasingly controversial—and environmental groups, this week, are leading an aggressive charge to put a stop to biofuels.

'No Way to Make Them Viable'

"The biofuels route is a dead end," Dr. Andrew Boswell, a Green Party councillor in England and author of a recent study on the harmful effects of biofuels, told *Spiegel Online*. "They are going to create great damage to the environment and will also produce dramatic social problems in (tropical countries where many crops for biofuels are grown). There basically isn't any way to make them viable."

The evidence against biofuels . . . appears quite damning.

The evidence against biofuels marshalled by Boswell and other environmentalists appears quite damning. Advertised as a fuel that only emits the amount of carbon dioxide that the plants absorb while growing—making it carbon neutral—it actually has resulted in a profitable industrial sector attractive to countries around the world. Vast swaths of forest have been felled and burned in Argentina and elsewhere for soya plantations. Carbon-rich peat bogs are being drained and rain forests destroyed in Indonesia to make way for extensive palm oil farming.

Because the forests are often torched and the peat rapidly oxidizes, the result is huge amounts of CO_2 being released into the atmosphere. Furthermore, healthy peat bogs and forests absorb CO_2—scientists refer to them as "carbon sinks"—making their disappearance doubly harmful.

Indeed, the Stern Review on the Economics of Climate Change, released in October 2006, estimates that deforestation and other comparable land-use changes account for 18 percent of all greenhouse gas emissions around the world. Biofuels, say activists, accelerate that process.

A Gold Rush

"We are causing a climate catastrophe by promoting agrofuels," Greenpeace agricultural specialist Alexander Hissting told *Spiegel Online*, using his group's preferred term for biofuels. "We are creating a huge industry in many parts of the world. In Indonesia, something akin to a gold rush has broken out."

The European Union seems to have taken note of the gathering biofuels storm. The plan has noted that the 10-percent goal is dependent on whether "production is sustainable," as an EU PowerPoint presentation delivered to reporters on Tuesday [January 15] noted. The EU also wants to make it illegal to use biofuels made from crops grown in nature reserves or in recently clear-cut forest lands. Crops grown in places valuable as carbon sinks are also to be avoided.

But critics doubt whether such clauses, which call for acceptable fields to be certified, is enforceable. "At the moment, such certification systems are very incomplete and it is very unlikely that they will ever work," says Boswell. "The biofuel supply chain is incredibly complicated."

Increasing Concerns

Even EU scientists doubt whether the supposed benefits of biofuels will ever outweigh the costs. A recent report in the *Financial Times* cited an unpublished study by the Joint Research Center, a stable of European Commission scientists, as saying that the "uncertainty is too great to say whether the EU 10 percent biofuel target will save greenhouse gas or not." It noted that subsidies in place to promote biofuels would cost European taxpayers between €33 billion and €65 billion by 2020.

Environmentalists say that emissions aren't the only serious problem created by the biofuel boom. Even crops grown in northern countries, like corn in the United States or rapeseed in Germany and the rest of Europe, harbor major dangers to the climate. Both maize and rapeseed are voracious consumers of nitrogen, leading farmers to use large quantities of nitrous oxide fertilizers. But when nitrous oxide is released into the atmosphere, it reflects 300 times as much heat as carbon dioxide does. Paul J. Crutzen, who won the 1995 Nobel prize for chemistry, estimates that biodiesel produced from rapeseed can result in up to 70 percent more greenhouse gas emissions than fossil fuels. Corn, the preferred biofuels crop in the US, results in 50 percent more emissions, Crutzen estimates.

[S]ome governments are beginning to listen to the chorus of criticisms.

'A Total Disaster'

Another issue receiving increasing attention recently is that of rising food prices as foodstuffs are turned into fuel. Price increases for soybeans and corn hit developing countries particularly hard. Indeed, there have already been food price riots in Mexico, Morocco, Senegal and other developing countries. While the price increases cannot be pinned entirely on biofuels, it has certainly played a role. In October [2007], the United Nations' Special Rapporteur on the Right to Food Jean Ziegler called for a five-year moratorium on biofuels to combat rising prices. Using arable land for biofuels, he said, "is a total disaster for those who are starving."

Slowly, it appears that some governments are beginning to listen to the chorus of criticisms. Last autumn, the Canadian province of Quebec announced that it would cease building plants to produce the biofuel ethanol. And on Monday, the UK's House of Commons Environmental Audit Committee called for a stop in the increase of biofuel use. "Biofuels can reduce greenhouse gas emissions from road transport. But at present, most biofuels have a detrimental impact on the environment overall," committee chairman Tim Yeo said, according to *Reuters*.

The European Union has reacted with anger to the UK report. Andris Piebalgs, European commissioner for energy, told the *Guardian* that "the Commission strongly disagrees with the conclusion of the British House of Commons report."

The report, though, is music to the ears of environmentalists like Boswell. "We have been highlighting these problems for a number of years," he says. "Now it is time for the UK government to act on the committee report."

Organizations to Contact

The editors have compiled the following list of organizations concerned with the issues debated in this book. The descriptions are derived from materials provided by the organizations. All have publications or information available for interested readers. The list was compiled on the date of publication of the present volume; the information provided here may change. Be aware that many organizations take several weeks or longer to respond to inquiries, so allow as much time as possible.

Advanced Biofuels Association (ABFA)
2099 Pennsylvania Ave. NW, Ste. 100, Washington, DC 20006
(202) 469-5140
website: www.advancedbiofuelsassociation.com

The Advanced Biofuels Association (ABFA) is a membership organization comprised of biofuels companies interested in promoting America's development of and transition to biofuels. ABFA advocates for sound public policies that "are technology neutral, utilize sustainable feedstocks, and offer subsidy parity to ensure all viable advanced biofuels can compete with the benefit of a level playing field." The ABFA website features industry news, recent press releases from the association, and listings of upcoming events. It also provides access to a range of informative reference and educational material, like an atlas of biopower and biofuels plants across the US.

American Biofuels Council (ABC)
9655 S. Dixie Hwy., Ste. 116, Miami, FL 33156
(305) 409-4285 • fax: (305) 553-0513
e-mail: info@americanbiofuelscouncil.com
website: www.americanbiofuelscouncil.com

The American Biofuels Council (ABC) is a think tank focused on biofuel research, analysis, education, and development. ABC collaborates with government, private companies, and academia to craft solutions to the nation's energy challenges and provide advice and strategy to the biofuels industry. It strives to serve "as an information network that is fully equipped to educate the public, media, and elected officials about the true economic and environmental benefits associated with the production and use of biofuels." On a local level, the ABC counsels municipalities how to reduce harmful admissions, transition to cleaner, renewable fuel sources, and improve air and water quality. The ABC website features information on recent news and initiatives.

Energy Future Coalition

1800 Massachusetts Ave. NW, 4th Floor
Washington, DC   20036
(202) 463-1947
e-mail: info@energyfuturecoalition.org
website: www.energyfuturecoalition.org

The Energy Future Coalition is a nonpartisan public policy initiative that promotes and facilitates the transition to a new energy economy. The Coalition brings together business, labor, and environmental groups to identify new directions in energy policy with broad political support. It also work closely with the United Nations Foundation on energy and climate policy, especially energy efficiency and bioenergy issues. The Coalition publishes a number of reports and articles concerning American dependence on fossil fuels and the process of transitioning to alternative energy sources. It also provides information on green jobs and opportunities in a new energy economy.

Environmental and Energy Study Institute (EESI)

1112 16th St., NW, Ste. 300, Washington, DC   20036
(202) 628-1400 • fax: (202) 204-5244
website: www.eesi.org

The Environmental and Energy Study Institute (EESI) is an independent nonprofit organization concerned with formulating and promoting public policies that lessen America's dependence on fossil fuels and facilitate the country's transition to clean, renewable fuel sources. To this end, EESI collaborates with members of the US Congress and facilitates communication between the government and other stakeholders, including environmental groups, private companies, consumers, and the biofuels industry. EESI educates Congress and the public through independent research, policy papers, fact sheets, and newsletters, including the *EESI Update,* which offers updates on current programs and research, and *Climate Change News,* a weekly newsletter that covers the key climate science news.

Environmental Protection Agency (EPA)
Ariel Rios Building, 1200 Pennsylvania Ave. NW
Washington, DC   20004
(202) 272-0167
website: www.epa.gov

The Environmental Protection Agency (EPA) is a US governmental agency tasked with protecting America's natural environment and safeguarding human health. The key responsibility of the EPA is to write and enforce environmental regulations. Established in 1970, the agency also conducts environmental research, provides assessments on environmental problems, and offers education on environmental policy and practices. The EPA works closely with local, state, and tribal governments to offer feedback and guidance on environmental policies and problems. The EPA website includes issues of its monthly newsletter *Go Green!,* a listing of environmental laws and regulations, updates on recent programs and initiatives, transcripts of speeches, seminars, and testimony, and in-depth research on environmental issues.

Global Biofuels Alliance
1540 East Lake Rd., Erie, PA   16511
(814) 528-9067
e-mail: info@globalbiofuels.org
website: www.globalbiofuels.org

The Global Biofuels Alliance was established in 2010 to promote the increased production, distribution, and use of advanced and environmentally sound biofuels in world markets.

To meet that goal, it works with national and international legislators and policymakers to formulate policies that help governments and municipalities transition from fossil fuels to biofuels. The Global Biofuels Alliance also offers outreach and educational services to inform lawmakers, private industry, and the public on the benefits of biofuels. The group's website offers access to its recent press releases and background information on ongoing initiatives and efforts.

Institute for Energy Research (IER)
1100 H St. NW, Suite 400, Washington, DC   20005
(202) 621-2950 • fax: (202) 621-2420
website: www.instituteforenergyresearch.org

Founded in 1989, the Institute for Energy Research (IER) is a not-for-profit organization that conducts intensive research and analysis on the functions, operations, and government regulation of global energy markets. IER promotes the idea that unfettered energy markets provide the most efficient and effective solutions to today's global energy and environmental challenges. It publishes various fact sheets and comprehensive studies on renewable and nonrenewable energy sources, the growing green economy, climate change, and offshore oil exploration and drilling opportunities. IER also maintains a blog on its website that provides timely comment on relevant energy and legislative issues.

Natural Resources Defense Council (NRDC)
40 W. 20th St., New York, NY   10011
(212) 727-2700 • fax: (212) 727-1773
e-mail: nrdcinfo@nrdc.org
website: www.nrdc.org

Founded in 1970, the NRDC is an aggressive advocate for US wildlife and environment. The NRDC has played an integral role in writing and passing some of America's most stringent and effective environmental legislation, and it actively lobbies the US government to pass laws and regulations that will preserve America's wild areas, oceans, and indigenous animals.

NRDC works to find and implement solutions to the world's most pressing environmental issues, such as alleviating global warming, getting toxic chemicals out of the environment, transitioning from oil and fossil fuels to alternative sources of energy, protecting the oceans, saving wildlife and wild places, and improving China's environmental record. The NRDC website provides a plethora of information on environmental issues, including fact sheets, position papers, and reports, and it offers opportunities to get involved in environmental activism.

Union of Concerned Scientists (UCS)
2 Brattle Square, Cambridge, MA   02238
(617) 547-5552 • fax: (617) 864-9405
website: www.ucsusa.org

Founded by scientists and students at MIT in 1969, the Union of Concerned Scientists (UCS) is the leading science-based nonprofit working for a healthy environment. UCS utilizes independent scientific research and citizen action "to develop innovative, practical solutions and to secure responsible changes in government policy, corporate practices, and consumer choices." UCS publishes in-depth reports on several important issues: global warming, scientific integrity, clean energy and vehicles, global security, and food and agriculture. It also publishes the *Catalyst* magazine, *Earthwise* newsletter, and *Greentips Newsletter*.

US Department of Energy (DOE)
1000 Independence Ave., SW, Washington, DC   20585
(800) DIAL-DOE • fax: (202) 586-4403
e-mail: The.Secretary@hg.doe.gov
website: www.energy.gov

The US Department of Energy (DOE) is a government department tasked with advancing the national, economic, and energy security of the United States. The DOE also promotes scientific and technological innovation in support of energy security and crafts legislation aimed to make the US more energy efficient and independent. To that end, the DOE is active in the development of biofuels and provides news and information on that topic on its website. The DOE advocates for the development of other clean energy sources as well, including wind, solar, hydropower, and geothermal.

US Energy Association (USEA)

1300 Pennsylvania Ave., NW, Washington, DC   20004
(202) 312-1230 • fax: (202) 312-1814
e-mail: jhammond@usea.org
website: www.volunteersforprosperity.gov

The United States Energy Association (USEA) is an association of public and private energy-related organizations, corporations, and government agencies that promotes the varied interests of the US energy sector by disseminating information about and furthering the understanding of energy issues. In conjunction with the US Agency for International Development and the US Department of Energy, USEA sponsors the Energy Partnership Program as well as numerous policy reports and conferences dealing with global and domestic energy issues. USEA also organizes trade and educational exchange visits with other countries. It also provides information on presidential initiatives, governmental agencies, and national service organizations.

Bibliography

Books

Michael Brune — *Coming Clean: Breaking America's Addiction to Oil and Coal*. San Francisco: Sierra Clubs Books, 2008.

Mario Giampietro and Kozo Mayumi — The *Biofuel Delusion: The Fallacy of Large-Scale Agro-Biofuel Production*. London: EarthScan, 2009.

Mark Gibson — *The Feeding of Nations: Redefining Food Security for the 21st Century*. Boca Raton, FL: CRC Press, 2012.

Anthony Giddens — *The Politics of Climate Change*. Cambridge: Polity, 2009.

Neil Morris — *Biomass Power*. Mankato, MN: Smart Apple Media, 2010.

David Pimentel and Marcia H. Pimentel — *Food, Energy, and Society*. 3rd ed. Boca Raton, FL: CRC Press, 2008.

Julie Richards — *Biofuels*. New York: Marshall Cavendish Benchmark, 2010.

Frank Rosillo-Callea and Francis X. Johnson, eds. — *Food versus Fuel: An Informed Introduction to Biofuels*. London: Zed Books, 2011.

Darren Sechrist — *Powerful Planet: Can Earth's Renewable Energy Save Our Future?* Pleasantville, NY: Gareth Stevens Publishing, 2010.

Andrew Solway   *Renewable Energy Sources.* Chicago: Raintree, 2010.

James Smith   *Biofuels and the Globalisation of Risk: The Biggest Change in North-South Relationships Since Colonialism?* London: Zed Books, 2010.

Joshua S. Graff   *The Intended and Unintended*
Zivin and Jeffrey   *Consequences of US Agricultural and*
M. Perloff, eds.   *Biotechnology Policies.* Chicago: University of Chicago Press, 2012.

Periodicals and Internet Sources

Larry Bell   "Biofuels: Fields of Pipedreams," *Forbes*, November 8, 2011.

John Paul Cassil   "Blighted Harvest: The American Corn Ethanol Disaster," *Washington Times*, November 10, 2011.

Fredrik Erixon   "The High Politics of Biofuels," *IP Global*, November 1, 2010.

Todd Finkelmeyer   "It's Not Easy Going Green," *The Cap Times*, November 9, 2011.

Rana Foroohar.   "Big Oil Goes Green for Real," *Newsweek*, September 18, 2009.

Pete Harrison   "Europe Finds Politics and Biofuels Don't Mix," Reuters, July 5, 2010.

Clifford Krauss   "Ethanol Subsidies Besieged," *New York Times*, July 7, 2011.

Jim Lane — "Advance Biofuels Biostock—Who's Got Game?" *Biofuels Digest*, November 11, 2011.

Fred Magdoff — "The Political Economy and Ecology of Biofuels," *Monthly Review*, July–August 2008.

New York Times — "The Misguided Politics of Corn Ethanol," September 19, 2007.

The Oregonian — "In the Skies, Something's Cooking," November 10, 2011.

Martin Robbins — "Policy: Fuelling Politics," *Nature*, June 23, 2011.

Ken Root — "Ethanol: Love It or Leave It?" *High Plains Journal*, November 11, 2011.

Sara Sciammacco — "Corn Ethanol Subsidy: A Losing Proposition," *Environmental Working Group*, March 25, 2011.

Ronald D. White — "Biofuels, Wind Power Show Gains, but Hurdles Remain," *Los Angeles Times*, November 10, 2011.

Queenie Wong — "Biodiesel Industry Reaching New Heights," StatesmanJournal.com, October 31, 2011.

Index

C

G